FAMOUS PIONEERS

by
FRANKLIN FOLSOM

with illustrations by
JOSEPH PAPIN

HARVEY HOUSE, Inc., *Publishers*
IRVINGTON-ON-HUDSON, N. Y.

The Wilderness Mystery Series

by Franklin Folsom

Some Other Books by Franklin Folsom

Table of Contents

FAMOUS PIONEERS

Pioneer Spirit

THERE'S A STORY about pioneers that goes this way:

One day out in Nebraska a stranger met a pioneer named Jack who was standing by his covered wagon.

"Where's your home?" the stranger asked.

"Hain't got no home," Jack replied.

"Where do you live then?"

"Where do I live!" Jack said scornfully. "Where do I live? I don't live nowhere. I'm marchin' ahead of civilization."

"Well, where do you sleep?"

"Sleep? I sleep where I like on the prairie, drink out of the North Platte, eat jack rabbits and raw wolf. But it's gettin' too crowded for me, stranger. I heard a whole family is comin' up the river to settle about fifty miles below here. So I'm leaving for the West tomorrow. I can't stand the rush."

Then there was the old-time cowboy in New Mexico who explained why he liked to pioneer in the wide-open spaces:

"I'm thankful this is a country where a man can switch his tail," he said.

Some men loved the West because of its freedom and

11

wide-open spaces. To others the West seemed crowded from the very first; it was chock-full of puzzles that excited them.

The West was the right place for anyone whose head buzzed with newfangled ideas or questions. And if a man liked danger or action or surprise, the West was for him.

It took pioneers of all these kinds and more to live all the different kinds of life there was room for in the West. It was an immense and changeable place.

Two hundred years ago the West was simply the mysterious forest that lay just beyond the Allegheny Mountains. But soon people moved into this woodland and cleared the trees. This new frontier quickly became an old frontier. The West moved on to the west, and it kept on going.

That was the pioneer spirit.

This book gives samples of that spirit, beginning with the years just before the American Revolution and ending with the period right after the Civil War. The stories here offer glimpses of pioneer life during a hundred exciting years. Some of the tales are old favorites, but others are new in a book of this kind. It seems to the author that a book about pioneers ought to show a little of the pioneer spirit!

Daniel Boone

Daniel Boone

"INDIANS!" DANIEL BOONE WHISPERED to his friend John Stuart. "They've ketched us, John."

Boone and Stuart had been hunting and trapping in the Kentucky wilderness for seven months. In all that time they had not seen one Indian. But now they had run into trouble.

The next moment a war party of Shawnee horsemen had the two of them surrounded.

" 'Twas my own fault," Boone said to himself. He'd been careless — but also unlucky. The white men and the Indians had been coming up opposite sides of a little hill and surprised each other at the top.

The Shawnees looked in silence at the white men's dirty buckskin clothes. One look was enough. Those splotches and smears came from grease and blood. Plainly Boone and Stuart had been killing and skinning deer — lots of deer. And they had been doing it in the Indians' own private hunting grounds. Kentucky had always been an area where Shawnees and other tribes hunted. White men were supposed to keep out.

"Show us your camp!" the Shawnee leader ordered. He spoke English, and white men had named him Captain Will.

15

Boone hesitated. Back at his camp deerskins and beaver furs were piled high. Now Captain Will would certainly claim the skins and furs. His warriors brandished their tomahawks, and the white men had to move along or be killed.

Somewhere in the woods were five other men who had been helping Boone and Stuart with their hunting. Where were they now? Boone wondered. Could they come to the rescue?

BOONE TRIES A TRICK

Boone was a superb woodsman, and he could travel as silently as any Indian. But from now on he pretended to be very clumsy. He broke twigs, stumbled, and made a general racket in the still forest. It was a trick to warn his five helpers.

Just as he hoped, Boone's noise alerted his men. But they did nothing to save the six horses at the camp, or the hides and furs that Boone had been collecting. They simply ran away and hid.

Boone watched the Shawnees seize his traps, his fine muzzle-loading rifles, his gunsmithing tools, his horses. Then the Indians loaded the horses with several hundred buckskins, which were worth a dollar each, and dozens of beaver pelts worth a buckskin each — or, as people said then and still say now, a "buck" apiece.

"These are ours," Captain Will said sternly. "They came from our hunting grounds. Now, brothers, go home and stay there."

He handed Boone and Stuart a gun, moccasins to wear, a doeskin for patching them, and powder and shot enough so they could hunt for food on the long way to their homes in North Carolina.

"If you come back," Captain Will added, "the wasps and yellow jackets will sting you."

Daniel Boone saw the point to Captain Will's joke. He would be in for trouble with the Indians if he stayed here.

But Daniel was no man to give up easily, just because he was in danger. He had seen a great deal of this rich land called Kentucky. He loved it. Here was a place where a hunter and trapper could grow rich. Besides he had no intention of letting the Shawnees make off with everything. At least he would get his horses back. He and Stuart set out toward North Carolina along a well-marked trail known as the Warriors Path. But they did not go far.

That night they turned around and crept up to the Shawnees' camp. Stealthily they located four of the six horses and led them away. Then off they rode down the Warriors Path toward safety — they hoped.

CAPTURED AGAIN

At dawn the two white men stopped. Daniel Boone flung himself on the soft grass to rest. Stuart squatted down to fix a moccasin.

"What's that?" Boone asked suddenly.

A little noise had made him look up, and he found himself staring — at Captain Will! Behind the chief came a galloping band of Shawnees. And every one of them was laughing. What an idea, that two white men could expect to run off horses from under their very noses!

Captain Will tied a horse bell around Boone's neck. Then he said, "Dance, brother!"

Boone decided he'd better dance, and he did, while the Indians laughed even harder. Still, they made no move to harm their captives. Instead, they promised to let the white men go free again, in a few days. First they wanted to get the horses safely across the Ohio River.

"Very well," said Daniel Boone. But he didn't care to wait that long. Slyly he and Stuart escaped one night. And this time they took good care not to be recaptured. Nevertheless, Daniel remembered the warning about "the wasps and the yellow jackets." Never again did he camp near the Warriors Path.

This happened at Christmas time in the year 1769. Daniel didn't give up and go back to North Carolina. He expected his brother Squire Boone to arrive shortly with fresh supplies. Till then Daniel would keep out of sight and wait.

OUT OF THE WILDERNESS

Squire Boone did arrive with the supplies, and Daniel stayed on for two years in the wilderness. Then at last he started home to his beloved wife and children. He was happier than ever before in his life. He and his brother Squire had been successful. Two valuable shipments of hides and furs had already gone out safely over the trail. The money helped to support his family and to pay the debts Daniel owed. Now he had a third big batch of hides to sell. And he had found new country where he intended to settle down and live.

Before the Boones moved westward, Daniel helped to arrange a treaty with the Indians which allowed white men to settle in Indian hunting grounds. Then he led a whole group of families across the mountains to the land he loved. Starting along the Warriors Path, they carved a road for their wagons through the forests, and they called it the Wilderness Road.

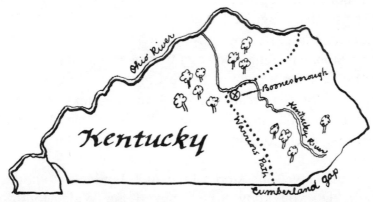

KIDNAPPED

Jemimah Boone, Daniel's daughter, felt quite safe in the new little village of Boonesborough which grew up on the bank of the Kentucky River. By the time she was fourteen, trouble with the Indians had died down. Her only worry one Sunday afternoon was a cut in her foot that she'd got from walking around with her moccasins off.

"Let's go for a canoe ride," Jemimah said to her friends Betsey and Fanny Calloway. "My sore foot hurts and I want to soak it in the water."

Betsey and Fanny paddled, while Jemimah steered and hung her foot over the side in the cool water. A little way below the village the canoe stuck on a sandbar.

Suddenly five Indians appeared from the brush and surrounded the girls.

The girls screamed and whanged the men over the head with their paddles. But the Indians only laughed and took them captive.

Jemimah recognized the leader of the party. He was Chief Stomach-Hangs-Down, a Cherokee who had visited her father's cabin back in North Carolina. The chief disapproved of the treaty which gave Kentucky hunting grounds to white men. Now he had joined some Shawnee warriors, spying on Boonesborough and planning for an attack later on.

"I shan't go one step with you," Jemimah told the chief. "Do you know who I am? I am Wide-Mouth's daughter." That was the name the Cherokees had given Daniel Boone.

"Are these your sisters?" the chief asked in perfect English.

Jemimah thought fast. "Yes," she answered. It might help if the Indians thought all three girls were daughters of the famous frontiersman.

Chief Stomach-Hangs-Down smiled cheerfully. For once an Indian was going to get the better of Daniel Boone! No harm would come to the girls. They would be adopted by the Shawnees. They might feel homesick, but nothing worse would happen to them.

Of course Jemimah didn't want to be adopted, and as soon as the Indians were on the trail with their captives, she thought of a scheme. She felt sure that by now people at home would have missed her. A rescue party would be out searching. Hoping they would hear, she cried:

"Oh! My foot! My foot!"

The Indians paid no attention.

"My foot hurts!" yelled Jemimah as loud as she could, and she began to walk slowly.

The chief gave her some moccasins. He also noticed that the girls' ankle-length dresses caught on briars. So he cut the skirts to half length and told the girls to wrap the cloth around their legs to protect them from scratches.

Gleefully Jemimah, Fanny and Betsey obeyed. This would give them just what they needed. They could leave threads and bits of torn cloth along their trail so that rescuers could follow them. But a whole day went by and no rescuers appeared. The girls pretended to be more and more tired. They hung onto bushes and broke off branches to leave more "sign" for pursuers to follow.

The Indians thought they were in luck when they found a stray horse. Jemimah, whose foot really did bother her, could ride now, and the party could move faster. But Jemimah had learned a trick or two from her father. She managed to go slower than ever by pretending she couldn't ride. Again and again she fell off. The Indians took time out to give all three girls riding lessons. Fanny tumbled off immediately. Betsey did a little better at first, then she, too, kept falling — even after the exasperated horse whirled around and bit her!

The Indians were patient. They felt sure they had avoided pursuit by walking down streams and following along rocky ridges where no footprints showed. By the middle of the third day Jemimah had lost all hope of rescue. The Indians killed a buffalo, built a small fire, and began to prepare their first cooked meal.

PURSUIT

Daniel Boone had been taking his Sunday afternoon nap when news came that his daughter Jemimah and her two friends must have been taken captive. Barefoot and wearing his Sunday pants made of cloth, he grabbed his rifle and set off on the search. Many other men from the village went with him. At last they discovered the "sign" left by the girls. But it was almost dark by this time. During the night someone raced home for Daniel's moccasins and his buckskin clothes that wouldn't get torn by briars. At dawn they were following the "sign" again.

By noon of the third day, Boone discovered a buffalo that had just been killed. He knew that he was close. The Indians would be cooking the meat beside the next stream. Now he had to be very careful. The Shawnees would kill the girls rather than give them up.

Noiselessly Daniel and his men crept close, fired on the unsuspecting Indians, and drove them wounded into the brush.

Chief Stomach-Hangs-Down would have been surprised to see how briskly the three girls walked home. Even Jemimah's sore foot no longer bothered her!

Daniel couldn't understand why the Shawnees had been hiding so close to Boonesborough that Sunday afternoon in July, 1776. But he soon found out. There was war between England and the Colonies. The British in Canada were now paying Indians to attack American settlements on the frontier. Although the people in Boonesborough didn't know it yet, the Declaration of Independence had been signed only three days before Jemimah was kidnapped.

DANIEL BOONE AND CHIEF BLACKFISH

The housewives in Boonesborough needed salt. Daniel had to get it, even though the trip would be dangerous, now that the British were paying the Indians to make raids on the white men. Besides, it was midwinter. Footprints would show plainly in the snow, and Indians could see them. Nevertheless, Daniel led thirty men to a spring of salt water that he knew about. There they camped and boiled the water down in kettles to get the salt.

One day Boone left the others at work while he hunted alone for fresh meat. Suddenly a party of Shawnee warriors surrounded him. They took him unharmed to their camp. There he discovered a hundred fully armed warriors, plus a number of white men sent by the British.

This could only mean that an attack on Boonesborough was planned. What could Daniel do? While he was thinking, the Shawnees crowded around him. He was such a prize captive that they all wanted to shake his hand!

"Howdy," Boone said to their chief, Blackfish.

"Howdy," Blackfish answered gravely. "My scouts have seen your men making salt."

Now Daniel had even more to think about. This big party of warriors would capture or kill the salt-makers.

Then they would fall upon Boonesborough. The British had offered a reward for any pioneer captives — or their scalps.

"I will arrange for my men to surrender, if you promise not to harm them," Boone said to Blackfish.

Blackfish agreed, and Daniel was sure he would keep his word.

Now Daniel said craftily, "You will have many captives. It will be hard to take women and children with you in this cold weather. I advise you to wait and capture Boonesborough in the spring."

Blackfish nodded. "I will leave the women and children till spring," he said. "But if the salt-makers do not surrender peacefully, you will be killed."

Boone went back and talked to his friends at the salt spring. They agreed there was nothing they could do but surrender. Through the snow they all marched off, prisoners of war, toward the British headquarters at Detroit.

BOONE BECOMES A SHAWNEE

Chief Blackfish took a great liking to Daniel Boone. He admired him so much that he refused to sell him to the British at Detroit, even though they offered a high price. Instead, he adopted Boone as his own son and treated him with kindness.

Boone pretended to become a good Shawnee. He allowed his long hair to be plucked out, Shawnee fashion, leaving only a scalp lock. Although he didn't particularly like this, there were many other things about Shawnee life that he liked and enjoyed. But when he saw his "father," Blackfish, preparing for a big raid on Boonesborough, he knew the time had come to escape. He must keep the Indians from suspecting his plan, and he did so in a very clever way.

When a group of hunters weren't looking, Boone slipped the lead balls out of their muzzle-loading guns, but left the powder in. He hid the bullets in a piece of buckskin under his shirt.

"Brothers, I am going home," he called to them suddenly. And he started off.

"You are not going!" Blackfish commanded. "If you try, I will shoot you."

Boone kept on walking.

True to his word, Blackfish picked up his gun. So did the others. As they fired, Boone held the piece of buckskin in the air and pretended to be catching the bullets. After the smoke cleared away, there stood Daniel unharmed. In his hand were the lead balls he had "caught" — the same ones he had stolen from the Indians' guns a few minutes before.

"Here are your bullets," he said to the astonished Blackfish. "Boone ain't going away."

The trick worked like magic — which the Shawnees thought it was. They grew careless and didn't watch Daniel as closely as they had before.

One day he saw his chance when all the men were out hunting turkeys. Only the Indian women remained in their camp. Boldly he seized a horse, said goodbye to his Shawnee "mother," and dashed for home.

Boone rode until his horse was nearly dead. Then he ran and walked the rest of the way. In four days he covered one hundred and sixty miles.

The warning Daniel brought saved Boonesborough. The people there had time enough to prepare for the attack. Although they were outnumbered seven to one, they managed to fight off the war party of Indians led by Canadian officers.

When the British lost the Revolutionary War, Indian
attacks on the settlements died down. Before long Boone
left Kentucky and followed the frontier west to the banks
of the Missouri River, where he lived to be almost eighty-
six years old.

In July, 1776 the people in the thirteen English colonies along the Atlantic coast were busy with plans for independence. The Revolution was starting. Many men who dreamed of exploring unknown lands of the West had to wait until the Revolution was over.

But men in the Spanish colonies on the other side of the continent were not yet thinking of revolution. Some of them had time to look into new places, and they hoped that by looking they might solve a big problem. Their problem was this: they had no direct way to travel between pioneer settlements in New Mexico and in California. Suppose a man wanted to go from Santa Fe to Monterey in California. He had to take a trail for a long way south into the Mexican state of Sonora before he met another trail that led north into California. In other words he had to make a trip that was much longer than the actual distance between the two places.

Spanish officials were not happy about this. Neither were Spanish churchmen. So it happened that a Spanish priest, Brother Escalante, with the help of the Governor of New Mexico, organized an expedition to look for a direct route.

Escalante

his astrolabe and looked at the stars to find out where he was on the face of the earth.

After a while the party came out of the mountains into flatter country. There they saw buffalo. The few longhorns that were left had grown very tough walking hundreds of miles on mountain trails. Buffalo steak was a welcome change from beefsteak!

The party turned west at a place that is known today as Dinosaur National Monument. Tremendous dinosaur bones lie buried there, but Escalante didn't know this. Anyway he wasn't interested in fossils from the ancient past. His mind was on just one thing: how to find an Indian guide who would take him in the direction of Monterey.

Perhaps the Spaniards would find help at the big lake they kept hearing about. Escalante's party went up over a mountain range. When they came down the other side they saw what they were looking for. A beautiful lake of fresh water stretched out in front of them. On its shore lived a band of Utes who were known as Fish Eaters.

"We do not know the place you seek," the Fish Eaters told Escalante, and they could not be persuaded to venture westward.

One man, however, did agree to lead the party off to the southwest. Old Miera looked at his compass and sighted the sun and the stars with his astrolabe and said Monterey lay to the southwest anyway, so the journey continued. Meanwhile winter approached and there were no more cattle to kill for food.

Along the way the explorers met little bands of Indians who seemed to be related to the Utes, but nowhere could they find anyone who would guide them. All the Indians said they were afraid of the terrible desert and the great mountains that lay to the west.

Escalante

BROTHER ESCALANTE SUSPECTED that the shortest route from Santa Fe to far-off Monterey would pass through the villages in the desert where Hopi Indians lived. But Escalante knew from bitter experience that Hopis did not welcome Spanish priests. It might be wise to detour around these villages, going either well to the south or well to the north of them. There seemed to be more streams and springs to the north. In addition, the Ute Indians who lived to the north had always been friendly to strangers. So Escalante made his plans to go northward.

He had no trouble getting volunteers to join the expedition. Another priest, Brother Dominguez, liked the idea so much that he decided to come along. Eight other men signed up. One was a tough old professional soldier, Don Bernardo Miera. He was good at making maps, and he carried a compass and an astrolabe — instruments that sailors used to steer by on the open ocean. These would surely help the explorers find their destination.

Four members of the party were young businessmen. The other three were servants, and one of these, Andres Muniz, had an important skill. He could speak the language of the Ute Indians.

These men, all on good horses, rode out of the Plaza in the little town of Santa Fe on the morning of July 29, 1776. They drove extra horses ahead of them. These were spares they would ride when their own horses grew weary. There were also many mules in the procession — all carrying heavy packs of food, cooking equipment, extra clothes, and presents to give the Indians along the way. After them came a herd of long-horned cattle. No one knew what hunting would be like on the trail ahead, and Escalante wanted to be sure the men would have fresh meat when they got hungry.

For many days the explorers followed a trail that led northward into the beautiful mountains of Colorado. Andres Muniz knew this trail. It had been used often by Spanish traders. But one day the trail ended. Andres Muniz could not tell which way to go. Escalante had to find a Ute who would act as guide.

The Spaniards now went every which way, not for a trail but looking for an Indian who woul them a trail. More than three weeks after leavin Fe they met the first Ute. He was not eager to le wives — he had three of them — but Escalante ga two hunting knives and several strings of glass For this pay the Ute agreed to lead the explorers a as far as a place where many of his tribesmen assembled. There someone might volunteer to a guide.

The Ute did as he had promised. Crossing rough, country, he led the procession of horses and mules cattle to an encampment of his people.

"Yes, I know the trails to the west," said one of Utes in the camp.

"So do I," said another and another.

"Then you will show us the way?" said Escalante.

"No." The same reply came from each of then "Fierce enemies, Comanches, are raiding in the countr along the trails."

"God will protect us from the Comanches," Escalante told the Utes, and he insisted on going.

The Utes gave the explorers fresh horses in exchange for the ones they had been riding. A guide reluctantly agreed to take the party as far as a big lake that lay some distance away. A small Ute boy eagerly joined the expedition. It would take him to his home which was beside the lake. He didn't have a horse of his own, so he rode sitting behind Brother Dominguez.

Day after day, week after week the explorers went north through magnificent mountains in western Colorado. Old Miera was sure of the direction because he kept an eye on his compass. More than once he got out

Should the expedition try to go on anyway — or should it turn back?

The explorers faced this question and had to answer it in a hurry. Snow was beginning to fall, and the party was almost out of food. Except for snow, when it fell, there was almost no water to be found.

Don Bernardo Miera, who was old enough to be the father of any other member of the party, said, "We must not turn back!" Then he added with scorn, "I can get to California. Can't you?"

But the younger leaders thought they should give up and go home. They had learned a tremendous amount about the country and the Indians who lived in it. With this information they could plan another expedition that would be successful. But if they went on now — and died before reaching California — all they had learned would go to waste.

The party was divided. Some agreed with the daring old soldier Miera. Some sided with the more cautious priests.

There seemed to be no way to settle the dispute except by drawing lots. They did draw. To Miera's disgust the decision was to return to Santa Fe.

Some men believe that Escalante and Dominguez fixed the drawing in such a way that their side could not lose. But whether or not the decision was fair, it probably was fortunate. Many later pioneers, who had much better equipment, died of hunger and thirst in the desert of southern California. Many others died of hunger and cold in the Sierra Nevada Mountains farther north.

However, the Escalante party did not reach safety merely by turning away from these dangers. In order to get home the explorers had to cross the Colorado River. They did not have time, before heavy snows came, to go back upstream where it was easy to cross. But just ahead of them, the river ran through a great canyon, which was the biggest, most dangerous hole anywhere in the world.

The Indians said it was impossible to climb down to the bottom of the canyon — except in one place. Even if white men did reach the bottom, they would die if they tried to cross the river. It raced between the canyon walls faster than a man could run. And if somehow the white men did manage to cross, they could not climb the canyon wall on the far side.

Since this one crossing seemed to exist, Escalante made up his mind to find it. The information was vague, and no Indian would show the Spaniards the trail. They headed for the river without a guide. On the way they found country so rough and wild that no roads have yet been built through most of it.

Very deep, very steep, very dry side canyons led down into the canyon. Escalante tried one after another. None of them led to any spot where it was possible to cross the river. The explorers had a hard time finding water in the side canyons. They ran out of food and had to kill and eat some of their horses.

At last they found one route that seemed practical. It was practical — for men on foot. In one place the trail narrowed and led across the face of a cliff. A horse or a mule with a pack on its back could not possibly squeeze along it.

"Take the packs and saddles off the animals," Escalante ordered.

Still the way was too narrow. The men had to get out their axes and chisel out the solid rock to widen a path for the animals to walk on.

One by one the horses and mules crept along the narrow trail to safety. Then men then tied lariats to the packs and saddles and lowered them down the face of the cliff. Finally, the animals, packs and men were all together again. But they still had to cross the rushing river.

After a long search they found a spot where the water seemed shallow enough. Two of the servants who were good swimmers led the way. The other men followed. Before night filled the bottom of the deep canyon, the whole party had struggled through the swift, muddy water.

"We have done it!" the men shouted. Then for sheer joy the priests, with all the others, loaded their guns and fired off shots of triumph.

The ten men stopped with the few horses they had left and rested a while on the bank of the river. Then, somehow, they all got up the south side of the canyon. They had accomplished the last of the three "impossible" tasks the Indians had told them about: They had climbed down into the canyon, crossed the river, and climbed up and out.

Dangers were not over, but good luck stayed with the party. They crossed another desert without dying of thirst. For some reason Hopi Indians let the hated Spanish invaders pass their villages without harm. Very weary, but still very much alive, all ten men reached Santa Fe on New Year's Day, 1777. And on that day at least, even old Miera probably forgave the priests for choosing to go home.

The expedition had not reached Monterey, but it had traveled 2000 miles and discovered what western Colorado, central Utah and northern Arizona were like. The explorers had studied a huge area which no pioneers had ever seen before. And what Escalante and Miera reported about the country helped other men cross it later. Another important part of the world had become known.

While Daniel Boone explored the southeastern part of the continent and Escalante looked over the Southwest, other men were interested in the Northwest. There was a very special reason for their curiosity. No one could say for sure whether all the Northwest was land or whether part of it was ocean. Many men hoped, and believed, that a waterway of some sort ran through that area connecting the Pacific Ocean with the Atlantic.

Many explorers looked for this stretch of water which would be a great help to ships. They sailed along the icy northern edge of Canada, searching for one end of the passage. They hunted for the other end of it along the sunny shores of California and the rainy coast of Oregon and Washington and British Columbia.

One name that men had for the passage they sought was the Northwest Passage. We know now that there is no such waterway, but when explorers started to look for it their search wasn't silly. They could not possibly know that it did not exist. No one had explored enough of America to know this.

What did lie between the two coasts north of the lands the Spanish had explored? Many people dreamed of finding out. One of these dreamers was a young man from New England, and his dream was big.

John Ledyard

John Ledyard

JOHN LEDYARD WAS A STUDENT at Dartmouth College in the year 1772. A number of his classmates were Indians, because Dartmouth was at that time a school where Indians could get an education without paying tuition. John liked the Indians he met in the log-cabin classrooms of the college. In fact, he liked them so much that he stayed away from classes for several months and went off to live in Indian villages that were far from any white settlement.

His Indian friends taught John many of their tricks of woodsmanship. For one thing he learned how to carve a big log into a dugout canoe. After he left the Indians, he made and paddled a dugout the whole length of the Connecticut River. No white man had ever made this trip before.

John enjoyed adventures. He loved to travel and explore, so it was no wonder that he became a sailor. Ships could take him to far places. One ship took him to England and there he heard that a famous explorer named Captain Cook was going out on an expedition to the Pacific Ocean. John joined the crew — which meant he joined the British Navy. Captain Cook's voyage was sent out by the British government.

For two years John sailed with Captain Cook, visiting strange islands all over the Pacific. Then in the spring of 1778 the ship explored along the northwest coast of North America. One day it dropped anchor in a place we now call Nootka Sound in British Columbia.

John peered eagerly at the trees along the shore. Some of them looked very much like the trees he had known in the woods in New England. But New England was much more than 2000 miles away. The familiar-looking trees seemed to say to John that the land must be all in one piece from east to west. Suppose solid earth really did stretch from the Atlantic Ocean to the Pacific — with no other ocean in between. That would mean a man could walk across America, with maybe a canoe ride now and then when he came to a lake or river!

John kept looking at the shore, and soon he saw people — dark-skinned men — come out of the woods. These men looked just like the Indians he had known so well back in New England.

Exciting thoughts raced through John's very handsome, very blond head. Indians might inhabit all of America! This meant he might have friends anywhere in America. These friends could help him if he wanted to cross the continent. John knew from his experience in the wilderness that Indians gave him help when he needed it.

The Indians who came aboard Captain Cook's ship in Nootka Sound brought black furs to trade. The furs came from animals called sea otters, and John thought they were the most beautiful furs in the world. Rich men in China thought so, too. They were willing to pay very high prices for sea otter pelts.

John had no great knack for business, but it was plain

that if he could start a trading post at Nootka Sound he might grow rich as a fur trader. And if he had lots of money, he could go on exploring, which was the thing he most loved to do.

For all these reasons, John Ledyard resolved to come back to Nootka Sound one way or another.

John was the first American from the Atlantic coast to see the Pacific coast. He was also a patriotic American. So it was odd that he got this view from the deck of a British naval vessel in the very midst of the American Revolution. But John had been at sea so long that he didn't know there was a war on. Luckily, he couldn't have picked a ship in which he had a better chance to avoid fighting against his fellow countrymen. The American officials knew that Captain Cook was gathering information that was important for the whole world. They knew also that he would have to sail on the Atlantic Ocean on his way back to England. So American warships on the Atlantic had orders to let Cook strictly alone if they should happen to meet him.

When Cook's expedition did reach England, John of course found out about the war. He was unhappy to be a sailor in the British Navy instead of the American Navy. For a while he managed to stay off ships that were fighting the Americans. Then one day his vessel dropped anchor in New York Harbor at a time when the British held it. Before he got mixed up in any battle, John deserted and joined his family and the American side of the war.

When peace came, John remembered his dream of returning to the West Coast. In Boston, in Philadelphia, in New York he tried to get up an expedition, but the United States was a new country and poor. American

businessmen had many problems. John could not persuade them to give him the money he needed.

Hoping to have better luck in Europe, he went from
place to place in Spain, England, France looking for a
ship that would take him to Nootka Sound. Several times
he almost had one, but each time something went wrong.
Then one day in Paris he met the famous American,
Thomas Jefferson.

Jefferson was deeply interested in John's talk of a fur-
trading post on the Pacific coast. Jefferson could see that
the trading post would be very important to American
business. And he was sure that an expedition right across
the continent would be equally important to the new
republic. It didn't really matter whether this expedition
went from east to west or from west to east.

"If you can't find a ship to take you all the way to
Nootka Sound, why don't you try another route?" Jefferson said to John one day. His idea was that John could
get very close to America by traveling overland eastward
across Russia and Siberia. At a place called Kamchatka
he would find Russian ships. These ships brought back
furs from the Russian trading posts that were scattered
along the northwest coast of America. John could surely
get to America on one of the Russian vessels. And when
he landed there, he could set out eastward, exploring the
vast land that lay between the Pacific Ocean and the
Atlantic.

This idea appealed to John, and he set out as soon as
he could, with only a dog for a companion. It was winter
by the time he reached Sweden, but John thought the
cold weather was lucky. It meant that thick ice ought
to form on the water between Sweden and Russia, and if
there was ice he could walk on it. He could walk to

Russia. This would save the cost of a boat fare, and saving was important because he had almost no money.

The distance John would have to walk was not very great. His bag was light. He did not even carry a gun, but he did have one bit of equipment — a peace pipe! He wanted to have this ready to smoke with Indians when he reached America.

Luck soon turned against John. Out on the ice he suddenly came to open water. The only way to get to the other side was to go twelve hundred miles around the Gulf of Bothnia to the north.

John went back and began to walk along the chilly shore. Seven weeks later he reached the other side of that small stretch of open water!

In Russia, John hitchhiked. He got rides with soldiers and with men who carried the mail. They drove clumsy wagons or sleds pulled by three horses. The rides were

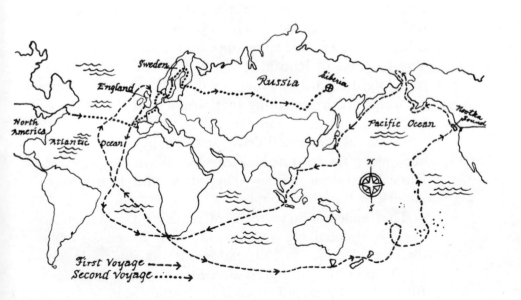

rough and the weather was cold. But everywhere the people along the way greeted John with warmth and generosity. They gave him food and shelter and clothing and sometimes even money which he very much needed. Part of the way he had the company of another traveler who spoke English. But most of the people he met could speak only Russian or some Asian language.

Stubbornly, week after week, month after month John Ledyard went eastward—toward America. Then one day when he had traveled nearly 6000 miles in Russia and Siberia, soldiers suddenly appeared and arrested him. The Empress of Russia, it seems, had begun to suspect that John Ledyard was some kind of spy. She was afraid he would learn something that would hurt the business of Russian fur traders in America.

As fast as they could drive, John's captors rushed him back along the road he had traveled. When they reached Russia's western border they made the heartbroken American leave the country.

That ended John's dream of reaching the American West by hitchhiking around the world in the opposite direction. He died in 1789 before he was able to do any more exploring. He never succeeded in being a pioneer fur trader. But he did succeed in another way.

John Ledyard made an important discovery about
men. In Siberia he saw many tribes that reminded him
of American Indians. The people looked like Indians.
They lived in much the way Indians did. John was sure
that the Siberians and the Indians were related. He went
on from that idea to another. He felt sure that the Indians must have come from Asia. No man had ever had
this idea before. Nowadays all experts on the subject
agree that John Ledyard was right. The Indians did come
from Asia.

Thomas Jefferson was a representative of the United States government in Paris when he talked to John Ledyard about exploration. Later Jefferson became Secretary of State. Still later he became Vice-President. During all this time he remained curious about what lay between the Appalachian Mountains and the Pacific Ocean.

Jefferson learned from pioneers that a great forest stretched westward for hundreds of miles on the far side of the Appalachians. But what was beyond this forest? Only a few scattered white men lived as far west as the Mississippi. Even fewer had explored beyond it.

In 1793 a British explorer, Alexander MacKenzie, made very important discoveries about the northern part of this distant region. He traveled through the Canadian wilderness all the way to the Pacific Ocean. He was the first man to cross the continent, and Great Britain claimed all the land he discovered.

Jefferson thought that explorers ought to go out westward from the United States, so that the United States also could claim land. He dreamed of a country that would some day spread from coast to coast.

In 1801 Jefferson became President of the United States. Now he had the power to do something about his dreams of expanding westward. In 1803 he bought a huge area that was claimed by France. It stretched from the Mississippi River to the Rocky Mountains, and people called it the Louisiana Purchase. Much later this area was divided into states. It included most of Louisiana, Arkansas, Oklahoma, Missouri, Kansas, Colorado, Iowa, Nebraska, Wyoming, Minnesota, North and South Dakota and Montana.

The Louisiana Purchase was as big as all the rest of the United States in the year 1803. Jefferson doubled the size of the country when he added this Purchase. But what was in this new addition? Nobody knew, and Jefferson was curious. He also wanted to find out about the land that lay west of it. He wanted to know what was between the Rocky Mountains and the Pacific Ocean. An American sea captain had found the mouth of the Columbia River that flowed out of this area and into the Pacific. How far inland could ships sail on this river? How far was the head of the Columbia River from the head of some river that flowed into the Mississippi? If the distance was short, perhaps freight could go by boat up the Mississippi, then by wagon or packhorse overland to the Columbia, and by boat again downstream to the sea.

Jefferson wanted answers to his questions, and he also wanted to make sure that the Columbia River country — the Northwest — would someday belong to the United States. So in 1804 he planned another great project.

He organized an exploring expedition.

Lewis and Clark

Lewis and Clark

JEFFERSON KEPT THE PLANS for his expedition secret, although everybody — except the Indians — agreed that the United States owned the Louisiana Purchase. Americans could explore there all they wanted to.

The reason for secrecy was this: The expedition was to go *outside* United States territory. It would go into territory that Great Britain might claim. And if Great Britain knew about this American expedition, there might be trouble.

To carry out his plan, Jefferson picked the young man he trusted most in the whole country — tall, bowlegged Captain Meriwether Lewis. Then, because he knew there might be great dangers in the heart of America, Jefferson made a suggestion. He proposed that the expedition have a second commander in case anything happened to Lewis. Lewis agreed and wrote his red-headed friend, William Clark.

"Will you go?" he asked Clark. Together the two men would explore the Louisiana Purchase. They would cross it, and then go on to the Pacific Ocean. Along the way they would meet dozens of Indian tribes, and some of these might be hostile.

When Clark received Lewis' invitation he wrote this reply: "This is an amence undertaking fraited with numerous dificulties, but my freind I Join you with my hand & Heart."

Clark couldn't spell, and neither could Lewis, but both were skilled frontiersmen and remarkable leaders of men. If anybody could find out all about the new land that President Jefferson had bought, they could.

Even the Army, which prepared all the equipment for Lewis and Clark, was told a false story about where they were going. When the flatboat and the canoes carrying their supplies moved up the Missouri River past Daniel Boone's new home, neither Boone nor anyone else suspected what was going on. Lewis and Clark might have been ordinary traders. A great Newfoundland dog barked from the deck of their boat. One man had a fiddle which he played every night while the rest of the crew danced. These things, together with a new-fangled air rifle which Lewis had, all proved in the end to be of real importance to the success of an amazing adventure.

Lewis and Clark set out from St. Louis, Missouri, in May, 1804. All summer and late into the fall, the men paddled and pushed and pulled the heavily laden boats against the current of the Missouri River. Then they built log cabins and settled for the winter near a Mandan Indian village in North Dakota.

GRIZZLIES!

All winter long the white men told the Mandan Indians tall tales. One of them was about a great animal back East.

"It has no mouth," they said. "It gets food only through its nose, by breathing in the steam from cooking meat."

The Mandans told stories, too. They spoke of an animal so huge and fierce that it took ten warriors with bows and arrows to kill one. After it had been skinned, two men could scarcely carry its hide. The white men would certainly meet these animals when they started up the river in the spring.

Of course, nobody believed the Mandans' stories. Lewis, after all, was a scientist. He had never seen or even read about a beast like this. But after the boats had traveled a little way farther upriver, Lewis quickly changed his mind.

Six of his men went ashore one day and crept up on a sleeping animal. Four of them confidently fired and hit it. Up rose a bear. He might have been ten feet long from the tip of his nose to the end of his spine, and he weighed as much as all six men put together. He was a grizzly, and he was merely angered by the four bullets. He

charged. Two more shots hit him and still he didn't stop. The men ran in a bunch to the river, then scattered. The bear paused, undecided which one to follow. This gave the hunters a chance to reload. Some of them fired again. Furiously the bear charged them. Two men leaped over the twenty-foot bank into the river. The grizzly followed, almost on top of them.

Only when the bear was slowed by the current did a man on shore stop him with a bullet through his brain. That was the only way of killing a grizzly with the low-powered muzzle-loading guns of those days.

Lewis himself got chased into the river once by a grizzly. "I must confess, I'd rather fight two Indians than one bear," he said. The Mandans had been telling the straight truth about the big, fierce animal up the river.

Day after day men had narrow escapes from bears. Even at night they wouldn't have been safe — except for Scannon, the enormous Newfoundland dog. When grizzlies tried to enter the camp, Scannon frightened them off with his enormous barks.

IMPORTANT PEOPLE

"Make friends with the Indians," President Jefferson had said to Captain Lewis when the secret expedition started.

Lewis took along great bales of presents for the Indians, to show that he wanted peace with them. But some things he hadn't counted on turned out to be equally important. One was the fiddle that Private Peter Cruzat played. Another was the square dancing that the other men did to Cruzat's music.

Almost every night the members of the expedition danced. Half of them wore white armbands to show that they were "ladies" in the squares. Indians, who loved dancing themselves, were fascinated by the white men's performances.

After the dancing, Lewis sometimes showed off his marvelous air rifle. It worked very much like our bee-bee guns. He had brought it along for emergencies — in case he ran out of powder. The Indians were delighted with its "magic" power.

Another asset was Captain Lewis' Negro slave, York. Indians had never seen a man with a black skin. They thought he must be painted. York himself was always amused when they tried to rub the color off with their fingers. The Negro dances that he did, and his feats of great strength impressed them, too.

Still another person in the expedition was even more important. This was a Shoshone Indian girl called Sacajawea or Bird-Woman. Lewis and Clark had hired Bird-Woman's French-Canadian husband to be their guide. In the end, she and her baby were ten times more valuable than he. The sight of a woman and a baby convinced Indians along the way that this was no war party.

SMOKE SIGNALS

"Look there! Another smoke signal!" Clark exclaimed.

"I cannot understand it," Lewis replied. "The signals mean that the Shoshones know we are here. But why are they hiding?"

Clark shook his head. For more than two thousand miles Indians had swarmed down to the river banks to see these strange men who had beards on their faces. Now, the one tribe they simply had to find was avoiding them. The success of the whole expedition depended on meeting the Shoshones and getting horses from them.

Lewis sighed wearily. He thought again about the two thousand miles they had come. Every inch of the way had been a struggle upstream against the treacherous Missouri. The last eighteen miles were the worst. Here they had been forced to carry their boats and supplies overland around the falls of the Missouri. It had taken his entire crew more than a month of heroic labor to travel just eighteen miles! And now failure lay ahead unless they could get horses.

High mountains rose in
the distance. The explorers
would have to abandon their
boats, and the men could not
carry everything on their
backs. Bird-Woman had told
them that her people would
sell them horses.

"We have no time to lose," Lewis said. "Winter will
catch us in the mountains. I must go on foot ahead of
the boats."

Clark wished he could go instead. But he had a badly
infected ankle. So with three companions, Lewis hiked
ahead over the cactus-covered flatland, following first
one trail and then another. There was plenty of Indian
"sign," but no sign of an Indian.

FRIEND OR ENEMY?

Lewis sent one of his men scouting far to the right
and the other far to the left. He and the third man
walked straight ahead. Every few yards he paused to
look through his telescope. Suddenly the figure of a
mounted Indian filled the lens.

"At last!" Lewis cried in great excitement. "Can you
see him? A horseman!"

Soon the horseman saw Lewis and stopped.

Above all, Lewis wanted not to frighten him away.
Bird-Woman had told him what to do. Quickly he slipped
his pack off his back and got out a blanket. He waved it
above his head and then laid it on the ground. In Indian
sign language, this meant "friendship." Lewis repeated
the sign three times.

The Indian saw the signal. But he also saw Lewis'
scouts who kept advancing. This looked suspiciously

like a trap. The two might close in on him from behind, while he went toward the man with the blanket.

The two scouts were so absorbed that they did not look back at Lewis for a prearranged signal to stop. In desperation Lewis shouted "Tab-ba-bone!"

The Shoshone began to back up.

"Tab-ba-bone!" Lewis cried again, moving forward.

The Shoshone hesitated a moment longer, then suddenly wheeled his horse and galloped off. Only later did Lewis discover what his mistake had been. He thought he was shouting the Shoshone word for "white man." But he mispronounced it. What he actually said was a word that meant "stranger" or "enemy"!

No wonder the Shoshone was suspicious of a man who signaled "friendship" and then cried "enemy," while two others seemed ready to pounce from either side.

SUCCESS OR FAILURE?

Lewis was in despair. The Shoshone would probably warn his people to run away. That would mean no horses — and an end to the expedition. Or the Shoshone might come back with warriors. And that would mean the end of Lewis!

To prove he was friendly, Lewis built a large fire on a hilltop. No enemy of the Shoshones would advertise himself so plainly. He left gifts by the fire, then moved on.

Next day he came upon two women and a man. They, too, fled when he called "Tab-ba-bone!" Soon he found a well-marked trail, and beside it two women and a girl.

Immediately Lewis offered them presents of beads and a mirror. Then he pulled out some vermilion paint and smeared it on their faces. Bird-Woman had told him that this color meant "peace" among the Shoshones. Meantime, one of Lewis' scouts, who knew sign language, was explaining as fast as he could.

"Friendly white men want to go to the Shoshone village."

The women led the way. But word had already reached the village that strangers had captured the women. A Shoshone war party came dashing to the rescue.

Lewis stood face to face with sixty angry warriors armed with bows and arrows. Unless he did the right thing, this would be the end.

LEWIS HAS A PARLEY

Quickly Lewis dropped his gun. He walked boldly toward the warriors, holding only the American flag. Then the women came to his rescue. They gleefully showed the presents he'd given them. Lewis and his men were not enemies.

"Ah-hi-e! Ah-hi-e!" the Shoshones began to exclaim, meaning, "Glad to meet you."

One by one the warriors embraced the white men, rubbing their greased and painted cheeks against the strangers' bearded faces. Lewis wished he could shake hands instead.

"I got tired of their national hug," he told Clark later.

But there was still more Shoshone etiquette that had to be observed. Lewis lit the peace pipe he had brought and passed it around. Then everyone went to the village. Here Lewis had to sit down and take his moccasins off while he talked to the chief. This was a Shoshone way of promising to tell the truth. It meant, "May I walk barefoot the rest of my life if I tell a lie." This was no country in which to go barefoot. Sharp rocks and cactus plants were everywhere.

Lewis invited the Shoshones to go back to the river with him. There they would see his boats and other wonders — and a man whose skin was black all over.

Immediately the Shoshones stiffened up. Maybe Lewis

was no friend after all. He must be trying to lead them into an ambush. Again Lewis thought fast.

"Tell the chief," he said to the scout, "that surely there must be *some* warriors here brave enough to visit my boats."

He waited anxiously as the scout moved his fingers in the sign language.

"I shall go!" The answer came from the chief. Lewis had said exactly the right thing. The whole village decided to go along.

THE LONG LOST BROTHER

Meantime, Clark was worrying. What had happened to Lewis and the scouts?

Clark and Bird-Woman set out to look for them. All of a sudden Clark paused in complete astonishment. Bird-Woman, walking ahead of him, broke into a dance. Then she signaled excitedly in sign language, sucking on her fingers. The sign meant, "People among whom I was suckled." She had seen the Shoshones coming with Lewis toward the river.

In even greater astonishment Clark watched what happened next. A Shoshone girl rushed toward Bird-Woman and embraced her. They were old friends. Lewis had stumbled upon Bird-Woman's own particular band of Shoshones.

When Lewis and Clark sat down to begin the ceremony of bargaining with the chief for horses, they asked Bird-Woman to interpret for them. More excitement — the Chief was Bird-Woman's brother! He hadn't seen her since the day five years before when she had been kidnapped by an enemy tribe.

Bird-Woman, who liked the whites, helped them buy horses from her people. The Lewis and Clark expedition could go on toward its goal.

Bird-Woman accompanied the explorers across the mountains. When they ran out of food she taught them to feed themselves on roots and berries and the hidden food-stores of little animals in country where there was no big game. Finally they reached the Pacific coast in November, 1805. The secret trip from St. Louis had taken a year and a half. The overland route to the Northwest had been opened.

The great dream of crossing America that had begun with John Ledyard, sailor, had been realized with the help of Thomas Jefferson, President.

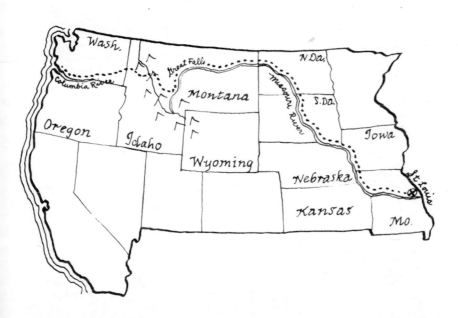

Often a new frontier became an old frontier in a very short time. Often an old frontier existed in one place while a new frontier was opening up in another. For instance, one summer night while Lewis and Clark were exploring in the Northwest, a boy had a strange adventure back in New York State where the frontier had been new only a few years before.

The adventure was important, too. It decided for the boy how he would spend the rest of his life.

George Catlin

George Catlin

GEORGE CATLIN WAS TEN YEARS OLD at the time of his adventure, and it started this way. He took down his brother's big rifle from above the fireplace and hung his little shotgun there in its place.

George hoped no one would notice that he had switched guns. He was not allowed to shoot the big rifle. That was probably why he couldn't resist the temptation to sneak it out into the woods so he could try his luck at deer hunting.

When he was safely out of sight of the house, George went to a spring he knew where the water tasted salty. Deer were supposed to like the salty water. George had heard they often came there in the late afternoon.

George had never fired a big rifle, and he had never shot a deer. Now he hoped to do both at the same time.

At the salt spring he found a hiding place behind a low rock. The rock was important. George could rest the gun on it. The long barrel was too heavy for him to hold steady unless he had some support.

When the gun was in place and cocked ready to fire, George lay flat on his stomach and waited. He waited and waited. Nothing happened. George began to feel uneasy, and as evening approached the time seemed to pass more and more slowly.

George grew restless. It was getting harder and harder to lie still and wait for a deer that might not come. George had just about decided to get up and go home, when he heard a sound. He heard it again, and again and again.

Footsteps!

The footsteps kept coming nearer.

He could not see anything at first. Then he glimpsed a dim shape. In a minute it grew clearer. There in front of him stood a deer — a buck.

The sight paralyzed George. He couldn't sight the rifle. He couldn't remember how to fire it. He just lay as close to the ground as he could and trembled with excitement.

Gradually he got control of himself and began to sight the rifle. Even with the barrel resting on the rock it wasn't easy to aim straight. The muzzle of the gun kept jiggling.

At last, though, he got a good steady view through the sights. He tensed his finger, ready to pull the trigger. Then —

A gun went off, but it wasn't his gun. The deer fell dead, but George hadn't shot it.

George was startled and confused. The next instant he saw something that amazed him even more. And it froze him with fear.

Out of the trees very close to him stepped an Indian, with his gun still smoking.

George couldn't believe what he saw. Everybody knew the last Indians had been driven from this part of New York State by 1790 -- more than fifteen years before.

But there in front of him, with dark skin bare from the waist up, was an Indian, and a big one at that.

George watched fascinated while the Indian hung the deer up in a tree, head down, so the blood could drain out. Then the Indian hoisted the whole big buck to his shoulders and walked away into the woods.

George hadn't dared to move till now, but when the Indian was out of sight, he fled. He ran all the way home as fast as he could — leaving behind the gun he had borrowed without permission. When he got to his house he realized he would be punished for taking the rifle and then losing it. But he was so excited by what he had seen that he couldn't keep quiet.

"I've seen an Indian! I've seen an Indian!" he shouted.

No one believed he was telling the truth.

George went to bed, excited, confused — and in disgrace.

Next day a man came to the house and told George's father that some gypsies were camping in a field on his farm.

"Those must be the people that George called Indians," Mr. Catlin said, and he took George to investigate.

There, not far from Mr. Catlin's wheatfield, was George's Indian sitting on a big bearskin, smoking a pipe. Near the Indian was his wife, and a daughter who was about the same age as George.

Mr. Catlin greeted the Indian and shook hands with him. It turned out the man could speak a little English. He said he was Great Warrior, an Oneida. His home was near Cayuga Lake a hundred and fifty miles away.

After Mr. Catlin had smoked Great Warrior's pipe as a sign of friendship, he told the Indian what George had said about seeing him shoot a deer.

Great Warrior gave a keen look at George, then he shook his hand.

"You are a good hunter," he said. Then he disappeared into the woods.

In a moment he was back bringing a chunk of deer meat.

"Your share," Great Warrior said and handed the venison to George.

Great Warrior then told why he was in the neighborhood so far away from his home. He had been in this very spot many years before at the time of the American Revolution. He was only a boy then, but he had come with his father on a raid against the American settlers. The Oneidas were fighting on the side of the British. This was partly because the British offered them rewards for killing Americans and partly because the Americans were stealing the Oneidas' land.

During the raid Great Warrior's father had seized a "gold" kettle. He had heard that gold was valuable and he wanted to take this kettle home with him. But the kettle was heavy so he buried it under a pine tree at this very spot. Great Warrior's father had never come back for his prize, and now the old man was dead, so Great Warrior himself had come. But Great Warrior had a problem. He could not tell where to look. The pine tree had been cut down.

When George heard this story he ran back to the house. There he picked up a brass kettle and brought it back to show to Great Warrior. George knew that a plowman had turned up this kettle at the very spot where Great Warrior said the "gold" kettle had been buried.

"Is this your kettle?" George asked.

Great Warrior studied it carefully.

"Yes," he said finally.

Great Warrior was very disappointed to find the kettle was made of brass. He had heard from traders that gold was very valuable. But Great Warrior was glad when Mr. Catlin gave him the kettle as a present. And he stayed on in his little camp by the wheatfield and paid the Catlins a good long visit.

Often George took food from the kitchen to Great Warrior and his family. George showed Great Warrior his arrowhead collection, too. He had a good one. He had found many of them in the fields nearby. There was even an iron tomahawk head in George's collection.

Great Warrior was very much interested in the arrowheads. He put shafts on them for George, and then put woodpecker feathers on the shafts. Then he made a quiver of deerskin to hold the arrows and finally he added a bow so that George could shoot them.

Great Warrior also put a new handle in the old iron tomahawk, and he taught George how to throw the tomahawk at a tree so that the blade would stick in the bark.

George had never been happier. Then one day Great Warrior said it was now time for him to return to his home. After saying goodbye, he started on his long journey.

The next morning George and his father found a big chunk of venison hanging in the tree by Great Warrior's camp. This was a present for George's parents. Sticking in the venison was a present for George himself. It was an eagle feather Great Warrior had worn in his hair.

This was a farewell to remember a long time. Then, later that same day only a few miles along on the trail to his home some men found Great Warrior's body. He had been shot and killed.

No one ever discovered who murdered Great Warrior, or why. No one knew what happened to Great Warrior's wife and daughter — or to the brass pot he had received as a present and was carrying back to his home. Only one thing was sure. An Indian had disappeared forever.

When George Catlin grew up he did everything he could to keep other Indians from disappearing. He spent his whole life trying to preserve the Indian world, in pictures at least. From 1830 to 1838 he traveled over huge areas of the West. He even went to Florida to visit the Seminoles. He went wherever there were Indians and he lived with them. He drew pictures of their ceremonies, their tools and weapons, their games, their hunts. He painted portraits of important chiefs. Always he tried to make pictures that were true to life, and many, many times he made pictures that were very beautiful.

George Catlin left nearly 2000 pictures in all. Because
of them and because of the books he wrote about Indians,
people today can know a great deal about life on both
sides of the old frontier. George Catlin saved all he could
of the world he loved so that others could enjoy it.

Families followed close behind the first pioneers who moved into the wilderness, and there were girls in these families, as well as boys. One of these girls was named Rebecca Wright. She was a Quaker and she started out from Baltimore, Maryland in 1805.

Rebecca Wright

Rebecca Wright

REBECCA HELPED LOAD THE big family wagon. Some of her cousins loaded other wagons. Then the Wrights — twenty of them — drove to a grassy place in the woods near their home in Maryland. There they spread table-cloths on the ground and sat down to a big farewell picnic with their Quaker neighbors. It was an exciting time, but a sad time too. There were so many goodbyes to say. At last, though, the big covered wagons started rolling westward.

When they reached Pennsylvania, the wagons followed a road that was really only a forest trail with a tree cut down here and there to make space enough for wagons to get through. All day, every day, the heavy wagons joggled and bumped and swayed. The motion made Rebecca feel seasick. It made her mother sick too — so sick that she had to stay out of the wagons and ride along behind on a horse.

At first Rebecca's family slept every night in an inn or in some settler's cabin. The welcomes in the cabins were always splendid. The people who lived there in the wilderness were lonesome. They liked it when strangers appeared.

The farther west the Wrights went, the farther it was from one cabin to another. In a few weeks there were no more cabins in which to stay. Now the travelers pitched a tent and slept in it even though the nights got very cold. The first time Rebecca tried to sleep on the ground she stayed awake all night. A flock of owls in the trees nearby kept up a chatter that sounded to her exactly like men talking to each other in a strange language. She was sure Indians were all around getting ready to attack.

The endless forest through which the wagon bumped along held many surprises — so many that Rebecca often forgot how seasick she felt. She could watch strange birds flying overhead, or see chattering squirrels race through the tree tops. Very often she sighted bright berries in the underbrush. When this happened she jumped off the wagon and started to pick. Many of the berries she found tasted wonderful, but some were bitter. Even these were fun, though, because they broke the monotony of joggling along in the wagon.

After two long months on the road, the Wrights reached the place in Ohio they were seeking. Ahead, behind a fence, was a cabin that belonged to relatives. The cabin was so far from neighbors that there was no

gate in the fence. There was no need for one. No one ever came to call. Rebecca's father and brothers had to take down the fence in order to drive up to the house.

Soon the Wrights had a log cabin of their own, far from any neighbors. There the whole family did all their living in one room. It was parlor, dining room, bedroom, kitchen and workshop too. Sometimes the room also served as a school. When Rebecca could get away from work she took lessons there from her older sister.

Rebecca was very fond of one job she had. When her father and brothers went out hunting for deer or looking for horses or cattle that had wandered off into the thick woods, she sat on top of a big fence post and blew a horn as loud as she could. The noise she made helped her father and brothers find their way home. The woods were so thick that it was very easy to get lost in them.

There was no telling what might come out of those dark woods, either. It might be a graceful deer, or a gobbling turkey, or a big clumsy bear, or a trotting wolf. It might even be something else — and once it was.

One day when Rebecca was alone, blowing occasional toots on her horn, three Indians suddenly appeared. They were out hunting in the woods which had always belonged to them, and they were curious about the strange noise Rebecca was making. Then they saw the cabin, and they were curious about that too. They walked right in, even though Rebecca hadn't invited them. She didn't know that this was considered perfectly polite behavior among the Indians, and she was frightened. She was also confused by the strange sounds they uttered and the strange gestures they made.

It took Rebecca a while to figure out that the Indians were really very friendly. All they wanted was some tobacco to put in their pipes.

There was no tobacco in the cabin but there was food, so Rebecca fed her guests. When they had eaten, the

Indians disappeared into the woods and that was the last
Rebecca ever saw of them. Perhaps they themselves
moved toward the west, trying to stay ahead of the white
men who kept moving into their hunting grounds.

In a very few years after Rebecca first settled on the
Ohio frontier, other settlers had cut down trees and
started farms all around. A steady stream of wagons now
came along the rough track Rebecca had followed. Today
autos on the Pennsylvania Turnpike rush through tunnels
in the very mountains that Rebecca crossed in a wagon.
And the big city of Dayton, Ohio, has grown up very
close to the spot in the wilderness where Rebecca once
sat on a fence post, blowing a horn.

The West moved far to the west before young Rebecca
Wright had a chance to do anything that could make her
famous among pioneers. But Rebecca was a pioneer.

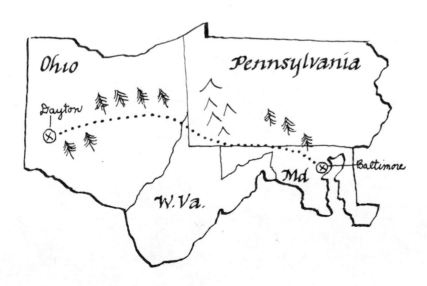

While pioneers like Rebecca Wright were moving into the part of the West called Ohio, Lewis and Clark were coming back from the Pacific coast. They had actually carried out the dream that John Ledyard had shared with Thomas Jefferson. They had crossed America — all of it.

The two explorers brought back knowledge that answered many questions that Americans had been asking about the continent on which they lived. But this information roused more curiosity than it satisfied. People now asked more questions about the West than they had ever asked before.

One man in particular was excited by the discoveries of the Lewis and Clark expedition. He had in fact been a member of that expedition.

John Colter

John Colter

"I'M NOT GOING BACK," John Colter told Lewis and Clark one day when the exploring party was on the way home. Colter, who had made the whole trip with the party, had fallen in love with the wilderness, and now he'd made up his mind not to leave it. So Lewis and Clark gave him permission to stay behind in the wild new country.

It was a dangerous life Colter had decided on, but he was full of confidence. He'd learned from Lewis and Clark how to get along with the Indians. And he was offered a job by a trader named Manuel Lisa who had a lonely little fort on the Big Horn River. Lisa did business with fur trappers and with Indians. He felt sure that a man who had Colter's experience would be just what he needed.

"I want you to go and make a deal with the Blackfeet," Lisa said. "They don't allow white men to trap in their hunting grounds, but I think you can arrange for me to trade with them."

"When do I start?" Colter replied. Nothing could have suited him better.

"On the way, you can visit the Crows and bargain with

81

them too," Lisa went on. He wanted all the trade he could get.

Full of enthusiasm, Colter set out. Up to now the Blackfeet had always traded with the Canadians. Perhaps he could win them over to trading with Lisa instead.

The scheme appeared harmless enough. John Colter had no way of knowing what terrible trouble it would bring to all the white men who came along later.

Traveling on foot, Colter hurried across the five hundred miles to Crow country. The Crows agreed to let Lisa come and trade. Then, reluctantly, they said they would guide Colter into Blackfoot country farther west.

Before long he found out why the Crows hesitated — and why he should never have asked them to go. Blackfoot warriors ambushed the Crows, who were their ancient enemies. Colter tried to stay out of the fight, but he couldn't. In the end he killed a Blackfoot and was wounded himself. Now he could never expect to go among the Blackfeet as a friend.

When his wound healed, Colter headed back for Lisa's fort, taking a shortcut through new country. And one day he came upon a sight that amazed and thrilled him.

Great fountains of water shot up out of the earth. Caverns in the rocks rumbled and growled. The air smelled of sulphur. In one place Colter saw a pool of boiling mud; in another, he saw springs hot enough to cook meat.

Later, when he told people what he had seen, they smiled and tapped their heads and spoke of "Colter's Hell." It was many years before anyone believed that he wasn't either lying or a bit crazy.

The place Colter had discovered was, of course, what we call Yellowstone Park.

BLACKFEET BECOME ENEMIES

"Go back to Blackfoot country in the spring," Lisa ordered Colter. "There's not one chance in a thousand that you'll meet a Blackfoot who recognizes you. I still think you can make a deal with them."

Colter wasn't so sure, but he set out anyway with another white man named Potts. One morning they were paddling their canoe along a river when hundreds of Blackfeet appeared on each bank.

"Come ashore!" the Indians signaled in sign language. At least they did not greet the white men with a shower of arrows. Still, Colter knew he had to make friends with the Blackfeet right away.

"Be careful," he said to Potts. "We must make no quick moves."

But Potts was so terrified that he forgot everything Colter told him. When the two men beached their canoe, the Blackfeet asked Potts for his gun. Instead of handing it over boldly, he tussled for it, jumped into the canoe and shoved off.

To the Blackfeet, this meant just one thing. The man was both a coward and an enemy. A moment later, he proved it. In a panic, he fired his gun, killing a Blackfoot. A cloud of arrows descended on him and he was dead.

From this day on, it would be war to the finish between white men and Blackfeet.

COLTER'S RACE

Colter had no reason to hope for his life, and yet he wasn't ready to give up. He knew that the Blackfeet would probably tie him to a stake and shoot him full of arrows. That was one way they had of dealing with enemy prisoners. Another way gave the strongest and bravest a chance to survive. The prisoner, naked, was allowed a long headstart in a race for his life. Warriors followed him with bows and arrows or lances. It was then a test of speed and endurance.

Now the Blackfeet were so angry at what Potts had done that they would scarcely want to give Colter a real sporting chance. But they were plainly discussing among themselves what to do with him. Colter waited, alert and tense .

"Can you run?" the chief asked at last.

"I'm no good," he said, hoping to make the Blackfeet think they would have no trouble catching him. Actually he was a wonderful runner.

The trick worked.

The Blackfeet took all his clothes — even his moccasins. Then they sent him three hundred yards off on the cactus-covered plain.

"Run!" the chief cried, and at the same time he signaled his warriors.

Colter ran like the wind. And he kept on running, in spite of the cactus spines that stabbed his bare feet. After three miles, he had left all but one of the warriors far behind. That one was gaining on him.

Still he ran — another mile, two miles. The warrior was right on his heels. Any second his lance might go through Colter's back.

Suddenly, nearly dead from exhaustion, Colter stopped and turned. The Blackfoot was so surprised that his own weary legs betrayed him. He stumbled and fell. Colter was on him in a flash, and the lance intended for the white man went into the warrior instead.

A river lay ahead. Colter ran for it. When the enraged Blackfeet reached it, Colter had already dived in and hidden himself in a beaver house. There he stayed all day long.

Finally the Blackfeet gave up the search, feeling sure he had drowned. Much more dead than alive, Colter crawled out of the beaver house and headed away from Blackfoot country.

Days later he struggled into Lisa's fort — still naked, cut and bruised, his feet a mass of cactus spines.

Colter had escaped, but for many years afterwards only the bravest — or the most foolish — white men sought to take beaver from Blackfoot streams.

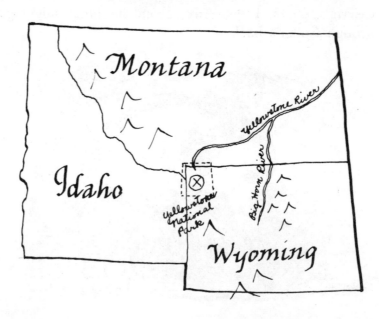

Lewis and Clark had found a northern route across America. But what about the vast stretch of plains and mountains that lay to the south? If any men besides Indians knew this part of the Louisiana Purchase, they were Spaniards. No men from the United States had explored it, though some were growing curious. One man who was curious had the power to do something about it. He was a general named Wilkinson. And this general had a special reason for trying to find out all he could about the Southwest. He wanted to take a huge chunk of land in that area away from the United States and set it up as a new country. Only a few people knew of Wilkinson's treacherous plans. Young Lieutenant Zebulon M. Pike had no idea what his commanding officer was really up to when the general one day gave him some very strange orders.

Zebulon M. Pike

Zebulon M. Pike

YOUNG LIEUTENANT PIKE FELT CHEERFUL in the early spring of 1806. He had returned safely from a long, dangerous exploring trip up the Mississippi River. Less than two weeks ago he'd led his men back into Army headquarters near the frontier town of St. Louis. Now General Wilkinson wanted to talk with him about a new assignment. Pike hoped he would be sent back East. He knew he wasn't a born explorer like Lewis or Clark.

"These are your orders," General Wilkinson said, handing Pike an envelope. Then he went on, "But I have other orders for you which cannot be written down."

The young lieutenant listened with growing amazement. He, Zebulon M. Pike, was asked to be a spy as well as an explorer!

The written orders were plain and simple. Pike was to go west through the Louisiana Purchase territory that the United States had recently bought from France. He was to make peace among the Indians of the Plains. He was to explore the headwaters of the Arkansas River, then find the headwaters of the Red River and follow it down to the place where it joined the Mississippi.

This section of the West was vast and unmapped. Nobody knew for sure which part of it belonged to the United States and which part belonged to Spain. Both countries wanted to claim as much of it as possible.

Spanish pioneers had been moving northward from Mexico, just as pioneers from the United States had been moving westward. Some of the Spaniards had settled in California, far away on the Pacific coast. But right now General Wilkinson wasn't thinking about them. He was interested in the areas we call New Mexico and Texas. He was also interested in Mexico itself.

"Find out all you can about the Spaniards and their plans," Wilkinson said.

"But, sir, I can't speak Spanish," Pike answered.

"I know that. But you speak French. You will find interpreters who know French, even if they don't know English."

"Very well, sir," Pike said.

"Perhaps the best plan would be to get yourself captured," Wilkinson went on. "If soldiers capture you, they will take you to a high officer in the Spanish Army. You will get a chance to travel in Mexico as a prisoner."

Pike looked a little doubtful.

"Naturally, the Spaniards will have to set you free before too long," the General went on. "You will be carrying these orders which tell you *not* to go into Spanish territory, but you cannot be blamed if you happen to lose your way in the wilderness. Good luck!"

Zebulon Pike didn't like pioneering. His expedition up the Mississippi River had already proved that. He would much rather spend his time where there were educated people to talk to and books to read. But he had a high sense of duty. He carried out orders — no matter how dangerous they were.

So, in July, 1806, Pike headed for the West. In his party were a doctor and less than two dozen soldiers who knew only that they were supposed to explore the Arkansas and the Red rivers.

Just before they left, Pike remembered to slip a certain book into his pack — a French grammar which he could study to refresh his knowledge of the language.

PIKE'S PEAK

"It looks like a small blue cloud, but I think it's a mountain," Pike said, holding a spyglass to his eye.

Later that day his whole party could see, without any glass, the snow-covered peak ahead, looming up in the west above the plains of Colorado.

"Three cheers for the mountains!" one man called, and they all gave three loud hurrahs. The blue mountain they cheered for that cold November afternoon in 1806, was of course the peak that now bears Pike's name.

So far, the trip had been hard but not very unusual. The men had pushed and pulled a keelboat up the Missouri River, then up the Osage River. Next they had traveled over strange prairie country on horseback to the Arkansas River. They met Indian tribes, and Pike persuaded them to stop fighting each other. All this was just what his written orders called for.

But Pike had failed to get captured by the Spaniards. He hadn't seen even one Spanish soldier, although he had followed the trail left by about three hundred of them who had gone far up into Kansas. The Spanish trail led into the mountains, so into the mountains Pike went. There, snow covered the soldiers' trail, and Pike had to find his way as best he could.

PIKE SAVES HIS MEN

The thermometer showed twelve degrees below zero. Pike's men wore moccasins, but they had no socks! Near the middle of January, nine of them got their feet badly frozen. And there had been nothing to eat for two days.

Now the commander of the expedition had to become a hunter in order to feed his men. In deep snow, Pike set out with three others. A whole day went by and they saw only one animal — a buffalo. Their shots failed to bring the huge beast down. Pike didn't know that a bullet from his low-powered gun had to hit a certain spot right behind a buffalo's shoulder in order to kill it. He wasn't a very good shot anyway. But he was determined.

"We cannot go back to camp without meat," he said. "The disappointment to the others would be more than they could bear."

And so, nearly freezing, the four of them spent the night out on a snowy, rocky hillside.

"Buffalo!" Pike said to his numb companions the next morning. He had sighted a herd about a mile away.

They crawled painfully through the snow and got within range. But again their shots only sent the animals lumbering away. It was four days since any of the men had eaten. They were almost too weak and cold to move. Even the stubborn, courageous Pike had given up all hope of living more than a few hours longer. And then he spied more buffalo.

With his last remaining strength, Pike managed to run a little way toward the herd without being seen. This time a lucky shot killed one. That night everyone, including the men with the frozen feet, had buffalo steak. Pike's expedition had been saved.

PIKE BUILDS A FORT

With no map to follow, often without food, Pike and a few of his men struggled through deep snow, up over a high mountain range. From the western side of it they could see a wide, beautiful valley with a river running through it.

"The Red River!" the men cried. All through these bitter weeks they had thought they were hunting for the source of the Red River. Now, they believed, their hardships had got them somewhere.

But they were wrong. What they saw was the Rio Grande at a spot not far from a Spanish settlement.

Pike talked things over quietly with Dr. John Robinson who had come along as surgeon for the expedition — and to help gather information about the Spaniards.

"Now it is up to you to make sure that the Spaniards find me," Pike said to the doctor. "You can go down to their settlements along this river. Say you saw me, but tell them you are on a business trip — you have to collect a debt for a friend. I'll build a fort to protect our party from Indians. When the Spaniards come, I'll be the most surprised man in the world to find that I'm on their territory. I'll be full of apologies."

SPANISH SPIES

While the doctor was gone, Pike had his men build a small log fort. Around it ran a moat filled with water. In order to get into the fort a man had to crawl along a plank over the moat and through a small hole at the bottom of a wall made of logs.

Now Pike was almost ready. He got out his French grammar book, which he had carried all the way during the terrible struggle through snow and over the high mountain pass. Then he sat down to polish up his French while he waited to be captured.

Before long two men on horseback appeared. Pike did his best to act friendly. At last he was able to lure them up close. One of them turned out to be a Spanish soldier. The other was a Pueblo Indian. Pike felt certain they were spies sent out from the settlements down the river, to discover whether Dr. Robinson was telling the truth.

CAPTURED AT LAST

The two mysterious horsemen left. Now Pike decided he'd better post a guard to watch out for the troops he

hoped would follow the spies. Meanwhile he kept studying his grammar book.

"Boom!" went the guard's gun one day — a signal that
Spaniards had been seen. Soon two officers appeared. To
Pike's delight they spoke French. He hadn't been wasting
his time! Behind the officers marched a hundred armed
soldiers. They had come, they said, "to protect" the
Americans from the Ute Indians.

Everything was very polite. Pike invited the two ele-
gant Spanish officers into his fort. He kept a perfectly
straight face while they got down on their bellies and
crawled along the plank and through the tiny opening
into the fort.

"Will you have breakfast with me?" he asked the
officers.

"Yes, thank you."

Pike gave them food he had got from their own Pueblo
Indian spy a few days before — venison, goose, cornmeal
mush, biscuits.

Of course, Pike pretended he was very much surprised
when they told him that he was on the Rio Grande, not
the Red River. The Spaniards pretended they wanted to

be very helpful. They would protect him with a large
force of soldiers who would guide him to the Red River.

A PRISONER OF SPAIN

From now on, everything happened just as Pike had
hoped. He was taken from settlement to settlement —
down the Rio Grande, then far into country south of the
river. He met the highest Spanish officials and learned a
great deal about the country.

All this time, of course, he was a prisoner. But Spain
didn't want to make the United States angry, so Pike and
his men were very well treated.

Finally, after a long trip down into Mexico, Pike was
allowed to go home and make his report to General
Wilkinson. He went by way of the Red River.

Zebulon Pike, who didn't really like pioneering, had
traveled an enormous distance and endured the greatest
hardships and dangers. And he had learned a great deal
about geography, which would help later pioneers. He
had even explored new country while he was a military
prisoner — which is quite a trick!

General Wilkinson failed in his plan to take the West away from the United States and make it into a separate nation. Pike's Peak was still in United States territory, but during the first fourteen years after Pike discovered it, no one climbed to the top of his mountain.

Edwin James

Edwin James

IN JULY, 1820, AN EXPEDITION under the command of Major Stephen H. Long approached the great peak. This party, which came along the foothills from the north, consisted of a small group of soldiers and a smaller group of scientists.

The soldiers rode in a strict order according to army regulations. The scientists rode wherever they pleased. They spent much of their time just seeing the sights — and there were plenty of these to see.

They watched the antics of prairie dogs — alert little creatures who lived in huge colonies. They followed the flight of handsome magpies through pine trees along the base of the mountains. They hammered off samples from great rocks that thrust up through the dry earth. Time and again they stopped to look at some flower. Then they dug it up, roots and all, and pressed it flat between sheets of paper so it would dry out and keep its shape.

These men drew pictures and took notes. They wrote down facts about streams and butterflies and clouds and weather. And while all these things were happening, soldiers in the line of march kept their eyes open and their guns ready. There was no telling when Arapahoes or

Cheyennes might decide that these white men — with their strange ways — were unwelcome intruders.

One of the scientists was very tall and slender. It was his job to be geologist and botanist for the party. He also kept the records and was historian. Besides all these responsibilities, he served as the physician and surgeon—and he was only twenty-three years old! The name of this remarkable young man was Edwin James. *Dr.* Edwin James.

When Edwin looked up at the snow-covered top of the peak, he liked what he saw. Here was a difficult problem to solve, and the harder the task, the more pleasure it gave him. No doubt about it. The job of climbing the mountain would be hard enough to satisfy him. The enormous mass of rock towered into the sky. No man had ever climbed a North American peak that high.

Before dawn on the morning of July 13, Edwin swung up onto his horse and headed for the base of the peak which rose at the very edge of the prairie. With him rode two companions. One was a twenty-year-old artist, Titian Peale. The second was an older man named Wilson, who was a trapper and hunter by trade. He knew nothing at all about Pike's Peak — except that men said it couldn't be climbed.

There were four others in the party. Two were mapmakers. They were only going as far as the base of the peak. Two other men would take care of the horses when Edwin and Titian and Wilson decided it was easier to hike than to ride. This decision came six hours after the trip began.

The three climbers continued on foot, and by noon they had already made a discovery that interested them greatly. They had found a tremendous spring bursting up out of the rock. A glistening white rim surrounded the spring, and the water sparkled and fizzed and gave off some kind of gas.

Edwin was curious about this gas. He wanted to know what it was. He didn't have much of a laboratory in the pack he carried, but he did have a box he had brought along because it might come in handy for something. Perhaps the box would hold some of the gas so he could make an experiment.

Edwin clapped the box shut above the fizzing water. Then he struck sparks with his flint and steel and set fire to some cedar splinters. These he put into the box. Would the gas explode? Or would it put out the flame?

Nothing at all happened. Edwin sniffed the gas. It was odorless.

There was no time to do anything more except wonder. Edwin would have to leave for later scientists the task of discovering that the gas was carbon dioxide — the same gas that fizzes out of soda pop. Right now the three men had to eat lunch. They set down their packs and took out huge chunks of deer and buffalo meat they had roasted. the night before. They cut off some slices for lunch. Afterward each man cut off ten or twelve pounds of roast to eat on the climb. Then they hung the rest in a tree and hoped they could find it when they came back down the mountain.

In addition to the meat, each man carried a pound of parched cornmeal, a pot in which to cook it, a blanket and a muzzle-loading gun with powder and shot.

Despite these heavy loads the men climbed steadily,

hour after hour. Often the rock underfoot was broken and loose. It slid and rolled down, slowing their progress. Sometimes the loose moving rock was right above the top of a cliff.

The men grew weary — very weary but when night came they were on a steep slope. They could not find any flat place big enough for a man to sleep on! To keep themselves from rolling downhill into a cold mountain stream that ran below them, the men built a barrier. They laid a log on the ground braced against two cedar trees. Then they made their beds on the uphill side of it. A single small blanket was not much protection against the night air. It was icy cold high on the mountain side, even in mid-July.

As soon as it was light enough to see, the three climbers wrapped their blankets around all the food and equipment they could spare and hung the bundles in a tree. The men climbed fast now — to keep warm.

Before long they climbed up out of the woods that covered the lower slopes of the mountain. For a short distance they passed through stunted, scraggly trees. Then they entered a strange world that none of them had ever seen or even dreamed of — the world above timberline. No trees grew here, but flowers flashed out everywhere — flowers of astonishing beauty — flowers that no botanist had ever seen. Many of these were intensely blue, as blue as the sky overhead. And Titian, the artist, had never seen a sky as lovely as the one above them now.

Wilson was too tired to care about the flowers or the sky or anything else. He could not keep up with Edwin and Titian, even though they stopped time and again to dig up strange plants or to watch curious little gray animals that looked like chubby squirrels that had lost their tails. Edwin wanted one of them for his collection of specimens. He aimed his gun and fired, but he had no luck. He had brought only big balls for his gun. They were for use in case of an Indian attack. What he needed to help him with his scientific collecting was some fine buckshot.

Discoveries followed one after another at a great rate. The closer Edwin and Titian got to the sun, the colder the air became. They had dressed lightly to save weight, and now they shivered at midday the minute they stopped moving.

Another discovery was this: High up on the mountain the air was filled with clouds of grasshoppers. This was a great puzzle. What could so many insects be doing up here? What did they find to eat?

Edwin and Titian struggled up and across large snow banks and into air that grew thinner and thinner. On every side were new plants. Edwin soon had to make a decision, and it was a hard one. He had to choose between collecting plants and reaching the top of the mountain. He chose the mountain.

At four o'clock that afternoon of July 14, 1820, Edwin James and Titian Peale reached the summit of Pike's

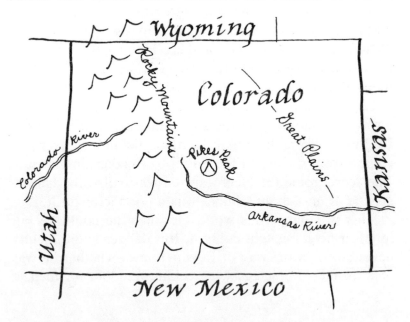

Peak. Soon after, Wilson joined them. Somehow he had found the strength to get back on his feet and overtake the younger men.

For as long as they dared, the three looked at the incredible beauty below. They saw clearly — as if they were looking at a big colored map — the Arkansas River winding out of the mountains and stretching in a thin line across the prairie. They took in more of America at one glance than any men ever had a chance to do before. Probably no pioneers anywhere ever had a more exciting reward for their labors. But the climbers had to stop marveling at the world spread out below them. They had to hurry down the mountain to rejoin their party.

When the whole exploring expedition was over and Edwin James had returned to the world of men, he continued to explore in one new way after another. It seemed to be in his nature to strike out in new directions. He pioneered, for instance, in the serious study of Indian languages. While he was a surgeon at army posts on the frontier in Michigan and Wisconsin, he collected all the facts he could about the languages of the first Americans, and he wrote articles about them. He also translated the New Testament into one of these languages — Ojibway. He wrote a book about life in two Indian tribes. Scientists today find it valuable.

Later Edwin James pioneered in still another way — a way that had to be secret, so it didn't make him famous. In Iowa, where he finally settled, he helped Negroes escape from slavery in the South to freedom in Canada. The secret route the Negroes used was called the Underground Railroad, and James was a conductor on it.

This was dangerous work. He knew he could be put in jail if he got caught doing it. But danger and difficulty never stood in the way of Edwin James, whether he was seeking facts for science, or seeking freedom for men.

The West was enormous.

While Escalante and Lewis and Clark and Pike and James and others adventured in the Rocky Mountains and beyond, there was still a great deal of pioneering to do in many places closer to the East. And it took all kinds of men to do this pioneering.

Some of the men on the frontier were as noisy as James was quiet. It is hard to separate the facts from the tall tales about them. But in a certain way even the tall tales are true. They show one kind of spirit that flourished on the frontier. And remember this: Some of the simplest facts of frontier life were so strange they were hard to believe, and some of the gaudiest lies that frontiersmen told sounded true.

So why should anybody bother with facts when it comes to a fellow like Davy Crockett?

Davy Crockett

Davy Crockett

DAVY CROCKETT WAS THE GREATEST BEAR HUNTER on the whole frontier. He and his dogs got seventeen bears the week before Christmas one year in the wildest part of west Tennessee. That was enough meat to last Davy and his family for a long time, and he could sell the hides for a good price. Davy was all set to celebrate the holiday, shooting off gunpowder on Christmas day, the way people did in those times.

But Davy and his little boy happened to stop in at the cabin of his friend McDaniel. Now McDaniel was a greenhorn, and Davy found he had no meat for Christmas.

"Come along," said Davy. "We'll just get you an eternal great fat bear."

Davy *hoped* they would. "It's turned mighty cold," he said to his little boy. "Maybe the bears have gone to house." Which meant they had crawled into warm holes to hibernate till spring.

Even when his dogs couldn't smell a bear, Davy was such a good hunter that he could find one anyway. He looked high in the trees. At last, in one big oak, he saw a hole. Below it were marks of bear claws.

"There's a bear in there," said Davy.

"How do you know?" McDaniel asked.

"He clumb the tree but he didn't come down."

"What makes you so sure?"

"When bears go up, they don't slip a bit. But when they come down, they make long scratches with their claws."

Just then the dogs began to bark, and away they went like a thundergust. Davy knew they had found a bear that hadn't hibernated yet. He and McDaniel rode off, killed the bear, then came back to the hollow tree where they'd left Davy's little boy. The boy was chopping away on the tree with his tomahawk.

But the bear didn't wait for the tree to fall before he woke up. The knocking roused him, and he poked his head out of the hole.

"Thar he comes!" Crockett hollered.

McDaniel caught up his gun. He fired at the bear. As soon as it touched the ground, the dogs were all around it in a roll-and-tumble fight. Bear and dogs in a squirming heap went down the hill. Davy ran after them, and while the dogs were a-wooling away on it, he put his gun against the bear and killed it. Then he and his little boy and McDaniel went home for Christmas.

By spring Davy had killed a hundred and five bears.
That's a lot of bears for one man. People got to talking
about Davy Crockett, and the more they talked the bigger
the stories grew. Some folks said that he salted his bear
steaks with hailstones, peppered them with buckshot and
fried them with streaks of lightning. They said he tamed
a thirty-seven-foot alligator and used it for a bench in
front of his cabin. They said he had such a powerful grin
that he didn't need to shoot small game at all. He just
grinned at possums and raccoons, and the critters would
give up, then and there.

DAVY CROCKETT WINS A BATTLE

The real Davy Crockett was just as popular with his neighbors as the stories about him were. Many of his friends had seen him in action in the War of 1812, and they knew he was brave and quick and a good leader.

When the war broke out, the British persuaded a group of the Creek Indians to attack an American settlement on the frontier and murder every man, woman and child in it. Crockett knew this kind of thing had to be stopped. He joined the army under General Andrew Jackson.

Davy fought in one battle to defend two hundred friendly Creeks from an attack by eleven hundred Creeks who were on the British side. In another battle, he helped to save the American army from ambush. It happened this way:

Davy, with some other scouts, was riding along at the rear of the army. That was where General Jackson suspected trouble would come. Jackson was right. All of a sudden, a thousand Indian warriors began to give it to the American troops, "as hot as fresh mustard on a sore shin." Some of the soldiers and their officers fled.

Davy and his scouts had just started to ride across a river. They turned their horses and charged straight into the middle of the Creek warriors who were confidently giving their blood-curdling yells. But Davy surprised and confused them. They couldn't believe such a tiny band would dare to attack. Davy galloped on and split the Creek army in the middle. The two halves ran in opposite directions. With Davy and his scouts chasing them, the warriors melted away among the hills. Crockett's handful of men had saved General Jackson's whole army.

THE COONSKIN CONGRESSMAN

At last when the war was over, Jackson signed a peace treaty with the Indians. The treaty took away half of the Creeks' land, as punishment because they had helped the British. But Jackson promised the Indians they could live forever on the land that they were allowed to keep. Davy thought this was fair enough.

Later on, General Jackson became President of the United States, and Davy's neighbors elected Davy to Congress. There had never been a hunter from the back-woods in Congress before.

Davy wasn't sure he'd like to live away from the wilderness. He didn't know how to read and write very well, but he figured he could learn — and he did, mighty fast.

At first people laughed at him and called him "the Coonskin Congressman." But Davy paid no attention. He was just as smart and just as fearless in Washington as he'd been in the wilderness. His motto was, "Be sure you're right. Then *go ahead*."

Pretty soon Davy decided that President Jackson was wrong about something. The President wanted to break his treaty with the Indians. He said they had to move away from the land where he'd promised them they could live forever. Davy knew the Indians well. He had lived among them peacefully for years. So he got very angry about the broken promise. He said it wasn't fair to make them move away. In Congress and everywhere else he did his level best to help them keep their lands. But he lost the fight. And when the next election came up, all the politicians were against him, so he lost that, too.

ON TO TEXAS

Davy decided it was time for him to go on to a new frontier.

Davy started out for Texas, where there was a lot of new land to settle on. Besides, the Texans were fighting a war to get their independence from Mexico. The idea of independence appealed to Davy. So in the year 1836 he decided to join the fighting.

People in Texas had already heard of Davy Crockett. They fired a cannon in his honor and asked him to a big celebration. Then and there he swore allegiance to the new, independent country of Texas.

"I will swear true allegiance to any future government that may hereafter be declared," the oath read.

"If you will add one word, I'll sign this," Davy said.

"What's that?"

"My oath must say 'future *republican* government,'" Davy answered. He was no man to support a king or a dictator. "We must govern ourselves as free men should be governed."

"We're with you," the Texans said, and the word *republican* was added.

When John Colter left the Lewis and Clark expedition to stay in the wilderness, he became a new kind of pioneer. He became a Mountain Man. Until about 1840 Mountain Men were the only people besides Indians who lived in or near the Rocky Mountains on the western edge of the Louisiana Purchase. This rugged breed lived outside United States territory, as well as inside it. Mountain Men went wherever they thought they might find animals to trap. They couldn't be bothered by little things like national boundaries or orders to keep out. Often their wanderings led them into territory that was Spanish. That is, it was Spanish in the years before 1821. After that the same territory was Mexican, because Mexico had won its independence from Spain.

Mountain Men roamed into the Northwest too — Oregon country, they called it. Nobody was quite sure who — besides the Indians — owned this part of America. Both the United States and Great Britain wanted it.

Wherever they pioneered, Mountain Men came to know the country well. They found all the ways to get through the mountains. They were ready to be expert guides when big official exploring parties came into the mountains and when pioneer miners and ranchers and farmers began to move west.

Imagine Daniel Boone and Davy Crockett in the Rocky Mountains and you have an idea what Mountain Men were like.

Mountain Men

THERE WAS ALWAYS A REASON why men pushed westward into new country. But in the 1820's one reason was very curious. Frontiersmen poured into the wilderness chiefly because of hats—men's hats! This is the story:

For some time, rich men had worn hats made from beaver fur. But each hat had to be made by hand. Then somebody invented a machine that could turn out the material for hats by the thousands, and they became very popular. Of course, the demand for beaver pelts became enormous. The supply of beavers in the West was enormous, too. So trappers went all the way to the Rocky Mountains to get them. In the Rockies — or the Stonies or the Shining Mountains, as people called them — fortunes in beaver pelts could be made. Only a handful of white men had ever been there. But soon hundreds of trappers were streaming in.

"Hooraw for the mountings!" they shouted, and they came to be known as Mountain Men.

Starting from St. Louis, some of them went in big parties, as employees of large fur companies. Others were free trappers who worked on their own and sold their furs to the highest bidder. All of them had to be adventurous and ready for every sort of hardship and danger.

INDIAN WARS

"Thieves and treacherous murderers!" That was what the Mountain Men called the Indians.

"Robbers and assassins," the Indians said when they talked about Mountain Men.

Both sides were partly right and partly wrong. How could that be? In the beginning, neither side knew much about the other. Take the business of horse stealing, for instance. Mountain Men had been brought up to believe that a horse thief was a criminal, a low kind of criminal. Indians, too, thought it was a crime to steal from members of their own tribe. But most of them felt it was a mark of great honor to be a successful stealer of horses from anybody *outside their own tribe!*

Most Mountain Men didn't understand this. So they called all Indians thieves.

The Indian custom of seeking revenge was another thing that Mountain Men didn't understand. Suppose a Mountain Man killed an Indian who was on a horse-stealing raid. The Indian's band or family then felt honor-bound to kill a white man — *any* white man. And among Indians it was a sign of great cleverness, not cowardice, to get revenge by shooting from the safety of ambush. White men called this a treacherous murder. Indians called it an honorable deed.

You can see how these very different customs caused a great deal of trouble. But that wasn't all. Many Indians thought that warfare was a kind of game which tested a man's skill and courage. Until they got new deadly weapons from the whites, they played the game in such a way that very few warriors were killed. The Mountain Men, on the other hand, believed that you fought a battle to win, no matter what.

The Indians were surprised at first by the deadly serious fighting of the Mountain Men who had guns and used them well. But soon warfare on the frontier changed from a very rough game, in which few were killed, to a life-and-death struggle. The Indians began to feel that they were fighting to save not only their lives but their hunting grounds — and, of course, they were. Both sides used every possible kind of trick to get rid of people they thought were enemies, or at least to frighten them.

HIT AND RUN

Three out of every five Mountain Men were killed by Indians. And nobody knows how many Indians were killed. The smart Mountain Men — those who lived a long time — were usually the ones who learned Indian customs and avoided fights, while taking every precaution. The Indians who tried to avoid fighting, and there were many of them, too, lost their lands anyway in the end.

It is often impossible to say which side was to blame in a particular fight. Usually it's just as hard to say who won a particular battle. Indians felt no shame about leaving a battle. They didn't see any sense in waiting until they were defeated. The war between the Indians and Mountain Men was a long series of hit-and-run fights.

The Indians finally lost because the soldiers and settlers who came West outnumbered them and killed the game on which they lived.

INDIAN LESSONS

"I never tasted bread for seventeen years," one old Mountain Man told his grandchildren. Maybe he was stretching things a little, but maybe not.

Mountain Men learned to live on meat, fish, and berries, the way the Indians did. In the beginning, fresh supplies came to them from St. Louis only once a year. And it was more important to have plenty of powder, bullets and things to trade with the Indians than to have flour for biscuits.

For bedding the Mountain Men used buffalo robes and bear skins. They made their own Indian-style clothes from soft buckskin, and their moccasins from buffalo hide, trimmed with colored porcupine quills. A long-tailed, fringed buckskin shirt and buckskin pants wore much longer in rough country than cloth did, because briars didn't tear the material easily. The one great trouble was that these clothes couldn't be washed — the buckskin would stretch all out of shape. In winter, the trappers in their dirty clothes were often miserable because they couldn't get rid of lice. But in summer they just laid their buckskins on anthills, and the ants ate the vermin up.

Indians taught the trappers to make their moccasins from buffalo-skin tepee covers that had been cured all winter with smoke from cooking fires. Many a greenhorn, who did not know better, used fresh buffalo hide. But if

he happened to go to sleep in wet moccasins, the uncured hide shrank as it dried, and he might wake up yelling with surprise and pain as his toes were pinched.

Unlike most Indians, a Mountain Man carried a muzzle-loading gun, a powder horn and a bullet pouch which also held the flint and steel he used for making a fire. At his belt he wore a steel tomahawk and a steel butcher knife in a stiff buffalo-leather sheath. All of his small things, such as a whetstone, pipe and tobacco, he put into a bag. He called them his "possibles," because they were of possible use. Finally, he had steel traps to catch the beaver, and horses to carry skins.

MOUNTAIN-MAN TALK

The Mountain Men had colorful words they used in their trade. Here are some of them:

Plew — a beaver skin. In the beginning, it meant an extra-good one, from the French word "plus," meaning more.

Foofaraw — beads, mirrors, ribbons, Christmas tree tinsel, or any other decorative thing that traders exchanged with the Indians for furs.

Booshway — a leader of a trapping party. The word came from the French "bourgeois," meaning trader or businessman.

Rendezvous — a big get-together and celebration held every summer when fur companies brought trade goods to the mountains and exchanged them for furs. Thousands of trappers and Indians met at the rendezvous where they loved to dance, hold wrestling and shooting matches, tell stories and exchange information.

Caravan — The fur companies' train of packhorses and mules that carried supplies across the Great Plains to the trappers' rendezvous in the mountains. After the rendezvous the pack animals took loads of furs back to St. Louis.

SIGN LANGUAGE

Mountain Men often had Indian wives, and they learned to speak the languages of various tribes, or at least the international sign language.

Sign language had been invented by the wandering tribes of the Plains who spoke many different tongues. In a territory that covered about a million and a half square miles, dozens of different tribes could talk with each other, using only motions of their hands. They could speak almost as clearly and as fast as if they used words.

The white men who bothered to learn sign language had a much better chance of surviving. One Mountain Man, Jim Bridger, was so good at it that he could spend a whole night telling jokes in it. For minutes at a time there would be a complete silence, while fingers were going nimbly. Then guffaws of laughter would fill the tepee.

Jim Bridger lived to a ripe old age!

Jim Bridger

Jim Bridger

"I'LL BET YOU'RE WRONG!"

"I'll bet I'm right!" Jim Bridger said.

Talk like this had been going on for days among the trappers. All of them were arguing about the Bear River, a most peculiar stream. It flowed north out of Bear Lake for a long way, then made a hairpin turn and flowed back south. Where did it end? Did it turn north again and meet the Columbia River? Did it turn west to the Pacific Ocean?

"There's only one way to find out," twenty-year-old Jim Bridger announced. "This hoss is going down it and see."

That was the way Jim always did things. He was curious about every inch of the West. If there was something he didn't know, he went personally to find out.

For a trip down the Bear, he'd need a boat, and he set about building one. He and the other trappers had learned from Indians just what to do. First he cut green willow branches and stuck the large ends in a circle in the ground. Then he bent the branches in toward the center and wove them together into a big basket.

Using rawhide thongs, he lashed the framework together. Next he stretched pieces of fresh buffalo hide over

125

the basket with the hair side against the framework. He fitted and stitched the pieces of skin carefully together and coated the seams with buffalo tallow. Finally, he built a small smoky fire on the ground inside the whole thing. As the fresh skin dried out, it pulled tightly together around the frame. The tallow filled every crack.

After the hide was cured in this way, Jim had a bowl-shaped boat called a bullboat. He carved himself a paddle and was ready to take off.

BRIDGER DISCOVERS SALT LAKE

The bullboat was small — just big enough to hold Jim's six-foot frame and his gun. He was an expert hunter, and he didn't have to take food along. He needed little but a gun, a knife and extra moccasins. There was no telling how far he'd have to hike back.

"You git back before snow flies," one of the older men advised him. The leaves of the box elder, cottonwood and aspen were already turning gold and orange.

"Be careful of yore skulp," another warned. There might be hostile Indians along the way who would try to take Jim's scalp.

Jim grinned and waved goodbye to the band of Mountain Men. In no time he was bobbing swiftly down the tumultuous Bear River. It was no easy trick to steer the round bullboat through the rapids and away from jutting boulders. Several hours of it were enough even for Jim's tough muscles. He was glad when the river passed out of a steep canyon and flowed more smoothly. Here he pulled the bullboat onto the shore and climbed to a high point for a look around.

Ahead of him the land flattened out. And far in the distance, perhaps twenty-five miles away, a huge body of water appeared. The sun glistened on its shining white shore.

Much sooner than he expected, Jim had seen where the Bear River ended!

Full of excitement, he ran back to his boat and paddled onward. The country grew more and more barren — almost like a desert. But at last Jim knew he'd reached the river mouth. And something strange was happening. His boat seemed to bob higher on the water. The whole place smelled peculiar, too.

More curious then ever, Jim scooped up some water in his hand. It tasted salty!

"By gawr!" Jim said to himself. "The Pacific Ocean!"

Jim had settled the argument with his friends. He'd found the end of the Bear River. But it wasn't the Pacific Ocean he'd tasted. It was the Great Salt Lake of Utah.

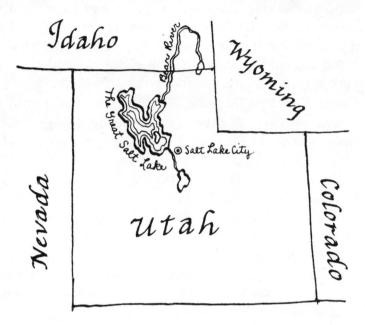

JIM HEARS NEWS

Jim Bridger expected his friend Jedediah Smith to join the other Mountain Men in their camp any day now. He had known Jed ever since the two of them started out together for the Rocky Mountains when they were teenagers.

No matter what happened, Jed always looked neater than most Mountain Men. He shaved and he kept his long hair evenly trimmed. Nobody dared to joke about this. All the trappers had great respect for Jed's courage and skill as a hunter. But they knew he had no sense of humor at all.

When Jed arrived, he brought news that sent Jim Bridger into a fever of excitement.

"I found a place that I'm sure is Colter's Hell," Jed said. "God has placed more wonders there than a man ever saw anywhere else on earth."

Jim knew that Jed was a deeply religious man. If he reported natural marvels, he must be telling the truth. Then and there, Jim Bridger decided to see this strange place for himself. And he did.

BRIDGER'S GLASS MOUNTAIN

Jim was fascinated by the wonders he found in "Colter's Hell." He tried to figure out what made the geysers spout. Why was a river icy cold in one spot and very warm farther downstream?

"I saw a mountain made entirely of black glass," Jim reported to his friends. "That's where the Indians get the stuff for those black obsidian arrowheads of theirs."

The other Mountain Men smiled. They thought Jim was telling tall tales. Before long, he heard one of them saying to a greenhorn: "Bridger's seen some mighty strange things in these mountains. One day he came on a heap of birds, all of 'em lying with their heads bashed in. He started to ride on and his horse fell down. Knocked out. He'd run head on into a hill of pure glass. The birds couldn't see it. Neither could his horse. They tried to go through, and of course they knocked themselves out."

Jim let this one pass. But the next time a greenhorn happened along, he got in there first.

"I was hunting last fall," Bridger said solemnly, "and I sighted an elk drinking at a stream. I fired. He never so much as lifted his head at the sound. I fired again. Still he didn't budge. I decided to move in closer. Something stopped me. I found myself smack up against a moun-

tain of glass. Magnifying glass, too. That elk I'd been
shooting at was on the other side — fifteen miles away."

AN ARROW IN THE BACK

No one could doubt one thing that Jim Bridger discovered in the Yellowstone area — fine beaver pelts. The
Yellowstone country was claimed by the proud Blackfeet, who fought fiercely to keep their hunting grounds
for themselves. But danger or no danger, Jim determined
to go back and get as many of the best plews as he could.

Other men had the same idea. One day Jim discovered
that rival trappers were trailing him, in order to find out
where his secret trapping grounds were. These men were
greenhorns, and at first Jim thought he could get away
from them. But sooner or later they always caught up.

Finally Jim's patience wore out. He headed away from
the land of geysers, hot springs — and good hunting. Before his rivals knew it, Jim had led them into an area
where there were no beavers at all. There, Blackfoot
warriors surprised one of the greenhorns, whose name
was Vanderburg, and killed him.

But soon Jim got into trouble himself. He and a party
of other Mountain Men met a large Blackfoot band.
The Indians made friendly signs and sent a small group
of warriors out with a pipe of peace. Jim, with an equal
number of Mountain Men, rode forward to meet the
Indians. The chief came on foot and unarmed, according
to the custom of peace conferences. But Jim feared a
trap. So he stayed on his horse and carried his gun.
Worse than that, he cocked his gun, and the chief heard
the telltale click.

Now it was the chief's turn to fear treachery. Instantly he grabbed Bridger's gun and pulled him from his horse. Blackfoot warriors, seeing the scuffle, came to their chief's rescue and sent two arrows into Jim's back. The chief leapt on Jim's horse and dashed out of range of the Mountain Men.

A day-long battle followed, with each side sniping at the other. There was no victory either way, but when the fighting was over, Bridger's men could get only one of the arrowheads out of his back.

The Blackfeet had made the arrowheads out of an old iron skillet. Jim wished they had used the black glass kind instead, because one of the iron points bent and stuck like a fish hook near his spine. There it stayed — a constant, painful reminder that Jim Bridger had made a mistake. He had rattled his gun at a peace conference. He couldn't blame the Indians for being suspicious. But he didn't leave the Yellowstone until he had a big pack of the very finest beaver pelts.

Jed Smith

Jed Smith

THE GREAT SALT LAKE was a great disappointment to Jedediah Smith. He'd hoped that the body of salt water that Bridger discovered was an arm of the Pacific Ocean. If it was, sailing ships could come in and pick up the trappers' furs.

Well, that idea was impossible. But what *did* lie between the Salt Lake and the Pacific? None of the Mountain Men knew. Jed Smith decided he had to find out. Maybe he'd locate good beaver trapping on the way. He might even find some kind of water route to the Pacific.

"I'll be back here next July," he told Jim Bridger and the other trappers in August, 1826. With thirteen men in his party, he left the Salt Lake area and headed southwest.

The farther he went the more desolate the country became. Game disappeared. Soon the men had only rabbits to eat — when they could find them. Sometimes Jed had to kill one of his horses for meat.

When they reached the Mojave Desert, thirst was worse than hunger. But finally, with the help of a friendly Indian guide, Jed crossed the mountains into California and saw the Pacific.

In those days, California belonged to Mexico. Jed was arrested as an American spy. But he managed to get his freedom by promising to take his men home.

The long journey back to Utah was even harder than the trip west had been. Nevertheless, Jed arrived, just as he'd said he would, in July, 1827. What he had found out had not made him rich, but he had filled in a great blank area on the map. And he knew there was wealth to be had in the wonderful California country.

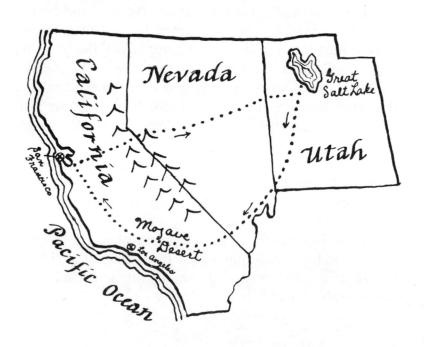

Joe Meek

Joe Meek

WITH JIM BRIDGER ON ONE of his trips to the Yellowstone area, went a famous trapper named Joe Meek. Now "meek" was the one thing you couldn't call Joe, but one day he did have to act that way for a while. He was setting traps alone when a party of Crows captured him. Oddly enough, the chief of the Crows was named The Bold.

"All white men are liars," The Bold told Joe, who understood the Crow language. "But if you answer my questions truthfully I'll let you live."

"I'll tell you the truth," Joe promised. There was nothing else he could say if he wanted to keep his scalp. He would answer the questions as he thought best and then hope that luck was with him.

"Who is the leader of your party?" asked The Bold.

"Jim Bridger, the man you call Blanket Chief," Joe answered truthfully. Then he added something he hoped would put the Crows off guard. "Bridger has forty men with him."

The fact was that Bridger's party was six times that large, including friendly Indians with their families.

The Bold had enough warriors in his band to surprise and scalp forty men.

139

"Where is Blanket Chief's camp?" The Bold demanded.

Joe told the truth again. He had to let Bridger know
that he was a captive, and he could do so only if the
Crows took him up close to the Mountain Men's camp.

The Crows prepared for battle and started on Bridger's
trail. Four days later Joe Meek read the sign language of
the Crow scouts who were out ahead. They had sighted
Bridger's camp.

SWAPPING PRISONERS

Now Joe's situation was desperate. The Bold took one
look at Bridger's camp and saw that Joe had lied about
the number of men there. Any minute the chief might
carry out his promise and have Joe killed.

But Jim Bridger had guards of his own on duty. One of them discovered the Crows and rode up to see what they wanted — just as the warriors were brandishing their tomahawks at Joe.

The Bold decided to wait a while. He was amazed at the sight of Bridger's camp, which included a thousand horses and mules, besides all the people. Perhaps it would be wise to act friendly and use Joe as an interpreter. So the chief ordered his warriors not to harm the captive — yet.

"Tell the white man to come here," said The Bold to Joe Meek.

Joe pretended to do as he was told. But what he really yelled was, "Stay back. Tell Jim Bridger that Joe Meek will be killed if he doesn't come and treat with the chief and get me away."

The guard was back at Bridger's camp in no time, and Jim quickly rode out on a big white horse.

"What tribe is it?" Jim called as he approached.

"Crows," Joe shouted back.

"Tell the head chief to send a subchief to talk to me," Bridger ordered.

The Bold sent a chief named Little Gun out ahead of his own party. Little Gun laid down his weapons, as was the custom when a peaceful talk was to go on. When he met Bridger, he embraced him as another sign of friendship. Then he and Bridger smoked a peace pipe together.

Meanwhile Joe still felt very uneasy. He saw the Crow warriors around him putting on war paint and preparing for battle. He hoped Bridger's men were doing something, too.

They were.

Five Mountain Men sneaked up and took Little Gun prisoner. Joe might be killed any minute for this treach-

ery in the midst of a peace talk. But Jim Bridger's men had moved quickly. When the Crows looked around, they saw a hundred guns aiming straight at them.

"Tell The Bold to exchange you for Little Gun," Bridger shouted.

Joe Meek translated the message. The Bold was furious, but he gave in.

"I cannot afford to lose a chief for one white dog's scalp," he growled.

Joe Meek walked toward Bridger's camp a free man, and Little Gun returned to his people, picking up his weapons as he went.

William Bent

William Bent

YOUNG WILLIAM BENT FELT plumb disgusted. Here he was — only twenty years old, already a "booshway"— leading a party of trappers into the mountains. But there was scarcely a plew to be found. Other men had beaten him to the beaver streams between the Great Plains and the Mexican town of Taos.

That wasn't his only trouble, either. He had brought along great bales of goods to trade with the Indians. And now Indians were even scarcer than beavers.

What should he do? A great deal of responsibility rested on young William. Little White Man the Indians called him, because he was short and very slender.

"We're bound to find Indians out on the plains," he decided. "Let's go."

He and his men set up a winter camp on the Arkansas River where the city of Pueblo, Colorado, now stands. Around it they built a stockade of cottonwood logs, in case wandering warriors decided to attack instead of trade.

One day, to Bent's delight, a party of Cheyennes approached on foot and cautiously entered the stockade. William smoked a peace pipe with them. He gave out presents. His fingers moved like lightning in sign language. But he couldn't sell them any goods. The Cheyennes were on a journey to take part in their favorite sport of stealing horses from the Utes. Since they were traveling light, they had nothing to trade.

Two of the Cheyennes were so fascinated with the riches that William had on display that they dropped out of the horse-stealing raid and stayed at the fort. They nosed into everything with intense interest, and the prints left by their moccasins could be seen everywhere in the dust.

William thought nothing of the footprints until a new party of Indians rode up to the stockade. Then he remembered that all Indians were trained from childhood to be expert trackers. The horsemen who had just arrived would know from the shape of the moccasin prints that Cheyennes had made them.

The newcomers were Comanches, powerful warriors of the southern Plains, and they had come out after Cheyenne horses—just as the Cheyennes were after Ute horses.

"Where are the Cheyennes?" demanded Bull Hump, chief of the Comanche raiders.

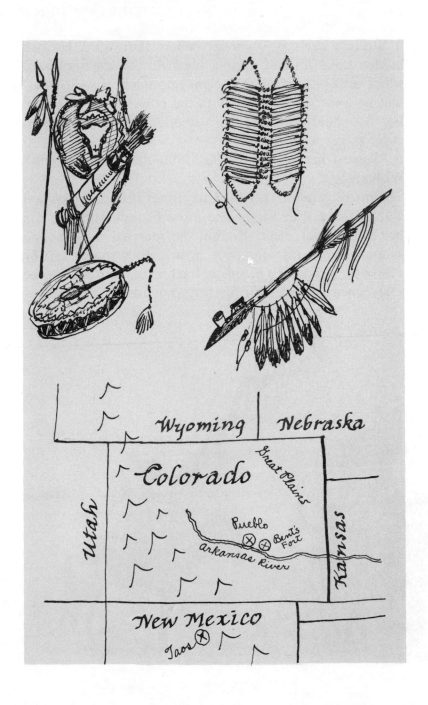

William knew well enough where they were. He had
hidden them himself among his bales of trading goods
when he saw the strange Indians approach. He also knew
that he wanted friendship with the powerful Comanches.
But he would not betray two unoffending Cheyennes in
order to get what he wanted.

"Some Cheyennes were here, but they have all left,"
William lied.

For this generous act the Cheyennes rewarded William
with lifelong friendship. The more he saw of them, the
better he liked them. In time he married a Cheyenne
woman. When his sons were grown, they fought on the
side of their mother's people in the hopeless struggle of the
Cheyennes to keep their hunting grounds for themselves.

A rendezvous was always the biggest event of a year for Mountain Men and traders. And the rendezvous in 1835, in the Green River valley, was more exciting than any that had been held so far. One reason was that a man named Whitman had come to it.

Marcus and Narcissa
Whitman

Marcus and Narcissa Whitman

"DOCTOR," SAID JIM BRIDGER, "could you do something about this arrowhead in my back? It tickles a leetle too sharp."

"If you can bear the pain, I'll take it out," Dr. Marcus Whitman answered.

Jim had stood all kinds of hardship, and he figured he could stand this too. No one had heard of anesthetics in those days. And no one on the western side of the Rockies had ever seen a doctor at a rendezvous either, until this year, 1835.

Mountain Men and Indians gathered around as Marcus Whitman prepared his sharp knives. It was only his second day at the rendezvous, and Whitman hadn't come to be a doctor — or to trade furs. He had come to talk to Indians about setting up a school and mission somewhere. But if there was medical work to be done, he could do it. And he did.

The point of the iron arrowhead was bent and stuck in some cartilage. That was why Jim's own men had not been able to get it out. The doctor had a job cutting it loose. But he worked skillfully, and Jim bore the pain in silence. At last Whitman pulled out the arrowhead and sewed up the wound.

White men and Indians both let out a great cheer. The
doctor hadn't counted on what happened next. Many
other men—Indians and white—had arrowheads in their
flesh, and Marcus Whitman was kept busy for days
operating.

Here was a man who could work greater wonders than
any Indian medicine man. Indians who saw what he did
invited Whitman to come and live with them and teach
them. This was just what he wanted. And Bridger was
so grateful that he acted as guide when the doctor started
out to locate a spot for his new mission.

NARCISSA WHITMAN

Next year there was an even bigger event at the rendezvous. Marcus Whitman returned, and with him came two figures that made the trappers rub their eyes. Two women — no doubt about it — trotted into camp riding sidesaddle. One was Narcissa Whitman, the wife of Marcus. The other was Eliza Spaulding, the wife of a man who had come to help at the Whitman mission.

No white woman had ever crossed the Rockies before. Indian women swarmed around the two pale-faced visitors and kissed them. Mountain Men rushed to shake their hands. Joe Meek arranged a celebration in honor of the two brave women who had made the long and dangerous trip and who still had a long way to go before they reached their destination in Oregon.

WHITMAN'S RIDE

Marcus built his mission in Oregon. Then, after six years there, he received a disturbing message.

"The mission committee has decided not to spend any more money on us," Marcus told Narcissa. "I have to go back east to Boston. I must persuade the committee to change their minds."

"You can't cross the Rockies in winter," experienced trappers told Marcus.

"But I have to save the mission," he answered. "People from the States are moving into Oregon. Now, white children as well as Indian need our school." And he started out.

"Wait till spring," a trader advised him when he reached the Rockies. "You can't cross in winter."

"If you don't travel, you can't get there," Whitman stubbornly replied.

Wearing a buffalo-skin overcoat and hood over his

buckskin clothes, he headed into the mountains. With him were two companions. They all rode Indian ponies. Mules carried their packs.

Soon the three men were lost in a blizzard. The snow was so deep that the mules and horses could climb only a short distance each day. More blizzards slowed them up. They ran out of food. One by one Marcus and his friends killed their pack animals and ate them.

At last they saw something ahead.

"The pass!" They had reached a high divide in the mountains. From now on they would be going down toward timber. But they could find no game to kill in the deep snow, and they were almost at the end of their strength.

Then suddenly it seemed to Marcus that the air had changed. He couldn't tell at first what the difference was. He took a deep breath. He sniffed.

"Smoke!" he cried. Smoke meant other human beings. Through deep snowdrifts, the three men followed the smell.

The smoke was real. It came from a cabin where some hunters were spending the winter. When Marcus regained his strength they gave him directions, and he struggled on to Taos, far to the south, where New Mexico is now. From there, he had a long cold ride east on the Santa Fe Trail. More than once he nearly froze to death on the treeless plains, but he kept saying to himself, "If you don't travel, you can't get there."

In the end he reached Boston. And saved his mission. Then he returned to Oregon and took many new settlers with him.

"If you don't travel, you can't get there," he kept telling them.

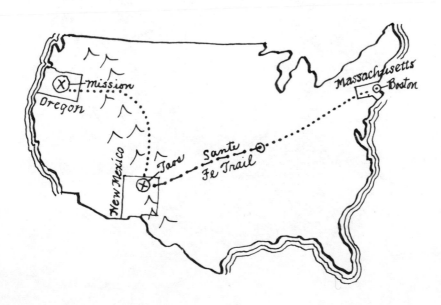

People were few and far between in the West in the 1830's. That was true of Indians. It was even truer of white men. Travel was slow too. In much of the West there was no water, so canoes weren't of much use. A man either rode a horse, or he walked. It wasn't easy for people to get together, but meet they did.

An astonishing number of the very early pioneers met each other at one distant point or another in the wilderness. Their trails crossed at trading posts or when they got together at a rendezvous. It was at the rendezvous of 1835, for instance, that Marcus Whitman met Jim Bridger.

At that same rendezvous there was also a quiet man in buckskin who was as short as Bridger was tall. A stranger like Whitman might have overlooked him in the crowd, but no Mountain Man would make that mistake. The slight fellow's name was Kit Carson.

Kit Carson

Kit Carson

SEVENTEEN-YEAR-OLD KIT CARSON spent all day every day in a saddlemaker's shop. He was what was called an apprentice. This meant that he had to work for almost no money while he was learning his trade — and he couldn't leave his job. He felt like a slave, and he didn't like the saddlemaker.

Kit lived in the little frontier town of Franklin, Missouri. Day after day he repaired saddles or made new ones for men who had wonderful tales to tell about adventures in the Rocky Mountains. And big wagon trains kept going through Franklin on the way to or from the romantic Mexican town of Santa Fe. It was more than Kit could stand to be cooped up at a workbench when there was an exciting world to explore in the West.

"I'm going to run away," Kit decided one day as a wagon train started for Santa Fe. No sooner had he decided, than he acted. That was the way Kit was.

He got a job herding horses for the wagon train. At seventeen Kit couldn't read or write, and he never learned to, but he became one of the most famous men in the West.

159

"TOO YOUNG FOR THE MOUNTINGS"

Fame didn't come to Kit Carson at once, however. At first he wasn't allowed to go with the Mountain Men who started their long journeys from Santa Fe or Taos.

"You're too small," one trapper would say. No doubt about it, Kit was small for his age, and he never grew much bigger.

"Go home to your mother," another trapper told him. "You're too young for the mountings." But Kit couldn't go home, although he loved his mother. His boss back in Franklin would make him work four more dreary years as an apprentice.

Finally Kit got his chance when experienced Mountain Men refused to join a party headed for Apache country. Oldtimers knew that Apaches killed white men on sight. They had been doing this ever since Spaniards had mistreated them years and years ago. But small as he was, Kit had no fear in him. He joined this expedition, faced the Apaches and helped drive them off.

Word spread of his courage and his skill with a gun. Kit found it easy to get other jobs, and soon he was one of the best trappers anywhere. He was welcomed on a party that went all the way to California in search of beaver. He trapped northward in the Rocky Mountains for hundreds and hundreds of miles. Mountain Men everywhere accepted him as one of them. They quit making jokes about his size or his youth.

HORSE THIEVES

Kit had a job one winter trapping beavers for a "booshway" named Gaunt. A band of friendly Arapahoes was camped nearby. Kit discovered that Gaunt was getting the Arapahoes drunk and buying their buffalo robes for almost nothing. One thing Kit never could stand was a cheat.

"I'm makin' tracks out of here," Kit Carson said.

Angrily he saddled his horse and rode out of the mountains toward the plains where he had heard William and Charles Bent were building a huge trading post called Bent's Fort on the Arkansas River.

The Bent brothers knew about Kit Carson and they hired him at once. Kit's first task was to take a dozen men out and cut logs needed to finish the big fort. One night in the logging camp he made one of his rare mistakes of carelessness. Instead of tying the horses close to camp, he let them loose to graze on the sparse dry winter grass.

Luckily, two Cheyennes, named Black White Man and Little Turtle, dropped in for a visit, and they didn't make the same mistake. They tied their horses near the place where they slept, and the animals were still there in the morning. But Kit's were gone!

Tracks in the snow that had fallen during the night showed that a large party of Crows had sneaked up on foot, captured the horses and ridden them triumphantly away.

"Crows!" Kit exclaimed in surprise. "What are they doing, a thousand miles from home? Come on — we'll git those horses back!"

Immediately he and a dozen men started on foot to follow the Crows. Black White Man and Little Turtle went along, too, riding their ponies.

The trail was easy to see in the snow, and by late afternoon Kit knew he had caught up with the horse thieves. A tiny wisp of smoke rose from a willow grove ahead.

"Spread out," Kit ordered the men. "And walk slowly toward the trees. We'll see what we'll see."

The two Cheyennes dropped back out of sight and rode their ponies around to the far side of the grove.

In a moment, Kit knew the Crows had seen his men approaching. A puff of steam went up in the grove where there had been smoke before. That meant the Crows had thrown snow on their small fire to put it out. Night was coming, and firelight would help the white men.

Kit wondered what the Crows planned to do next. Suddenly he found out. Sixty warriors, armed with bows and arrows and tomahawks, leaped yelling out of the grove and charged the thirteen white men.

"Fire!" Kit shouted. The Mountain Men blazed away with their guns.

As suddenly as they had appeared, the Crows slipped back among the trees. They saw no sense in standing out in the open to face men who had guns and who didn't scare easy. The way to fight men on foot was to charge into them on horseback. The Crows ran for their horses.

But the animals had disappeared! While the Crows had been on one side of the grove, preparing to surprise Kit and his men, Black White Man and Little Turtle on the other side of the grove had quietly run off all the horses.

It was the Crows' turn now to be afoot, facing men who had horses as well as guns. The warriors fled across the plains in the growing dusk. Kit and his tired men camped cheerfully for the night — but with a guard over the horses. Kit seldom made the same mistake twice.

KIT CARSON MEETS COMANCHES

Comanches were the best horsemen of the Plains. At least, they had the best horses. Young men of the tribe got their mounts — and great honors, too — by raiding the ranches owned by Mexicans in Texas and far south of the Rio Grande. No tribe was more bold and fearless, or more fiercely determined to keep its hunting grounds. Comanches wasted no pity on poachers they found in their country.

Kit Carson knew this. But he always went where he pleased and did what he pleased. One day he decided to hunt in Texas. He understood the risks, but he was fearless himself and a superb shot. And he trusted the men he chose to go with him.

One was Bill Mitchell who had lived as a Comanche for years and who still liked to dress Comanche style — that is, naked except for moccasins and a breechclout. Another was harum-scarum Joe Meek who made up in courage and skill what he lacked in caution. Then there were three Delaware Indians, all good shots and trained from boyhood to fight. The Delaware tribe, not so long before, had been pushed by white men out of New Jersey and Pennsylvania. All across the continent they had fought both white men and other Indians on whose lands they tried to settle.

Kit and these five men jogged along on their tough

mules over the treeless prairie, looking for buffalo skins, not scalps, but they felt ready for anything.

"Comanches!" Bill Mitchell shouted one spring morning. He had spotted a scout on a rise of land far ahead.

In no time, two hundred horsemen were charging across the prairie. Their screaming war cry told Kit this was no party coming to welcome the visitors and invite them to make themselves at home in Texas.

"Kill the mules!" Kit ordered. Each man slit the throat of his animal. Then all together they hauled the carcasses into a circle to use for protection.

The Comanches streamed on toward the six men who now scratched frantically at the earth with their knives to dig a better fortification.

"You three fire first," Kit said to the Delawares. "While you're loading, the rest of us will fire. We don't dare have all our guns empty at once." It took time to ram new powder and lead into the muzzle of a gun after each shot. Kit and his men would be helpless against Comanche arrows and lances unless some of them were always ready to shoot.

On galloped the magnificent Mexican horses. A chief rode out ahead. The three Delawares drew a bead on him. If he fell, it would frighten the Comanches much more than if three other warriors fell.

The Delawares took their time. Only when the chief was almost up to the little fortress did they fire. He rolled off his horse. The rest of the charging warriors swept by on either side, then wheeled and charged back. Kit, Bill and Joe brought down two of them.

Again the Comanches swept past. This time they paused, but too close. The Delawares got another warrior. And still not an arrow had touched Kit and his men.

SIX AGAINST TWO HUNDRED

Evidently the Comanches had decided to use their
lances. On they rode, but at the last moment their horses
balked! Not one horse would come close enough to the
dead mules for a warrior to thrust his lance. The smell
of blood frightened the horses off.

As the Comanches drew back out of range, Kit and
the others stood up insolently and jeered. Kit made it a
rule always to show that he wasn't afraid.

But the Comanches weren't through by any means.
Again and again they charged. Finally their medicine
man led an attack. Only when he fell did their confidence
waver. They decided to let the hated intruders suffer for
a while without water in the hot Texas sun.

From time to time, warriors rode out and circled the little fort that the six men kept digging deeper into the ground. But now the Comanches had grown more cautious. As each warrior circled, he slid over onto the far side of his horse, holding himself on with one arm through a loop of hair in the mane and one heel on the horse's back. From under his animal's neck he shot arrows toward the dead mules.

Kit and his men kept shooting, but they hit only horses now. The Comanches were getting smart. Finally they decided it wasn't worth risking any more horses or men. Away they went!

Kit's party waited to leave until early the next day. Traveling on foot at a steady jogtrot, they headed north out of Comanche country. They had to go eighty miles before they finally reached water, but Kit and his five friends made it.

Pioneers kept moving westward, and they kept wanting to know what lay ahead of them. Mountain Men could tell them a lot, but Mountain Men didn't study the land the way scientists do. They didn't draw maps and write reports that others could use. This was work for men like Lewis and Clark and Edwin James. There were other scientists too who went out on official expeditions to learn what they could about the wilderness. One of these had a special knack for exploring. His name was John C. Fremont. He was a good surveyor. He liked to study nature. He wrote very careful — and very interesting — reports. He was full of enthusiasm for the wilderness. He loved to live out of doors.

Fremont was a new kind of pioneer — a professional explorer. For many years he acted as the eyes of America, and America kept looking at the West.

Fremont studied with keenest interest one particular section of the West. It lay north of the lands that Escalante and the Spaniards had explored and south of the route that Lewis and Clark took across the continent.

In his purposeful wanderings between the Columbia River and the Colorado River, Fremont passed through much of Colorado, Wyoming, Utah, Idaho, Nevada, California and Oregon. He made four big trips and they took him over more of America than any explorer had ever seen before. It was no wonder that pioneers who followed Fremont had a name for him. They called him the Pathfinder.

The Pathfinder's explorations came at an important time for the West. They came when the United States was still growing in size. Fremont went into Oregon country, and Oregon became part of the United States. Fremont went into California while it still belonged to Mexico, and California soon became part of the United States.

John C. Fremont

John C. Fremont

TWELVE-YEAR-OLD RANDOLPH BENTON could hardly believe his good luck. Here he stood, this June day in 1842, on the deck of a little steamboat going up the Missouri River. Randolph was the youngest member of an exploring party, on his way to the Rocky Mountains.

He looked with interest at the buckskin-clad men on board. They would be his constant companions for months to come. Now and then his eyes turned to the handsome young Army officer, Lieutenant John C. Fremont, who had married his sister and who was in charge of the party.

"Do you know anything about the mountains?" Randolph heard Fremont ask a rather small stranger.

"Reckon I do. Why do you ask?"

"I need a guide to South Pass and beyond," Fremont answered. "The guide I hired has disappeared."

"I can take you to South Pass as easy as a beaver can smell bait."

Randolph followed Fremont around the deck and listened to the inquiries he made about the small stranger, whose name was Kit Carson.

"Know him!" one old fellow said. "Who don't? This

child may be dead if Kit Carson ain't the best trapper in the mountings."

"Know Kit Carson?" another grinned. "I saw him shoot up that bragging Shunar — the fellow they called the Big Bully of the Mountings. At the rendezvous in '35, Shunar had everybody buffaloed — Mountain Men, Arapahoes, everybody. Then he tried to cross Kit who was about half his size. They had it out in a fair duel on horseback. Kit's here, and Shunar's wolf bait."

FOR FREE MEN

It didn't take Fremont long to decide that Kit Carson was the man to guide the expedition. Kit had learned all about the mountains in his trapping days. But the fur trade was now almost a thing of the past. For one thing, the beavers were getting scarce. More important, men's fashions had changed. Silk hats were in fashion now instead of felt hats made out of beaver fur. So Kit Carson was glad for a job as a guide.

For months, Randolph Benton stuck close to the great frontiersman, and he learned how to track men or animals, how to sleep in the open, how to hunt buffalo, how to live among the Indians of the Wild West.

Everything about the trip was exciting, even the reason for it. Randolph knew that his father, the famous Senator Benton in Washington, had persuaded the Army to send Fremont to the West. Papa was interested in finding out all he could about the West, so that settlers could go there to live. He wanted the settlers to be men who worked their own farms, not slaveholders.

Right now Texas was asking to join the Union — with slavery allowed. Back in 1836, Davy Crockett had gone to Texas to fight, as he thought, for liberty. Whether he knew it or not, one reason why the Texans rebelled

against Mexico was a Mexican law making slavery ille-
gal. Many people didn't want to let Texas into the Union
until they could balance it with a no-slave state — or lots
of no-slave states — in the West. So this expedition was
part of a big plan to have the West settled by men who,
like Senator Benton, didn't want slavery to spread.

Fremont was just the man to find out about this vast
new country. He loved the wilderness. A daring, adventurous man himself, he soon learned Kit Carson's worth.
When this first expedition was over, he took Kit along
on more exploring trips to the remotest parts of the
continent, through great areas that even Kit had never
visited.

First Expedition - - - →
Second Expedition ...... →

DOING THE IMPOSSIBLE

It was February 1844, and the high Sierra Nevada Mountains stood between Fremont and California, which he was determined to explore.

"I'm sure we can get across," he said to Kit Carson, and he told his men to make snowshoes and sleds.

Wearing snowshoes, he and Kit scouted ahead. They zigzagged uphill for ten miles over snow that was anywhere from five to twenty feet deep. At the top of a divide, a great view to the west opened out in front of the weary pair.

"See that little mountain?" Kit pointed. "I remember it. Now I know exactly where we are." He hadn't seen the mountain for fifteen years, but he had an amazing memory. "We can make it. Look below. Grass for the horses."

Then began a terrific struggle. Men used huge blocks of wood on long handles to pound down the snow, beating a path for the horses. It was slow, exhausting work.

The weather grew colder. More snow fell. Food supplies ran out. They began to kill horses for meat. Finally they had to eat the expedition's pet dog. They fought their way on for a week — for ten days, just to cover the terrible ten miles up to the divide. Then they had to go down the other side.

Two men lost their minds temporarily, because they had taken more hunger and cold and danger than they could stand. But at last the weary party left the arctic weather of the mountains and came out into what Fremont called "the perpetual spring" of the Sacramento Valley. There he and his ragged men and starved animals rested and regained their strength.

This was a land much to Fremont's liking. His enthusiasm grew by the minute. Here was indeed a place where free Americans could prosper.

Americans who wanted a country that was big and strong — and where there were no slaves — remembered John C. Fremont in 1856. That was the year they started a new political party, the Republican Party. The founders of that party made Fremont their first candidate for President. Fremont didn't win, but his political pioneering led the way for Abraham Lincoln who ran as a Republican four years later and did win. Fremont turned out to be a pathfinder in politics just as he had been in exploration.

But this talk about Fremont and politics is getting ahead of the story. It was years earlier, in the 1840's, that he did his exploring. And it was in the 1840's that Americans by the thousands began to move into the West that Fremont had found. These pioneers followed trails that Fremont had used. Fremont for his part had very often followed trails that the Mountain Men had learned about from Indians.

Virginia Reed

The Donner Party

THIRTEEN-YEAR-OLD VIRGINIA REED enjoyed every minute of a trip she took in 1846. She rode her pony, Billy, all the way from Springfield, Illinois, to Bridger's Fort which was near the present border between Wyoming and Utah. While Virginia's mother rode in the family's covered wagon, Virginia often rode out far ahead with her stepfather, James. His mount was a beautiful race horse he called Glaucus.

Sometimes when she felt like it, Virginia galloped across the prairie looking for buffalo or swift little antelope on either side of the wagon train. She loved the Reeds' covered wagon, too, the fanciest one that had ever crossed the plains. It was so big that it had a roomy kitchen and a cookstove inside. And there were two stories under its canvas roof, with bunks upstairs for the family to sleep in at night.

The whole wagon train was headed for California, where Colonel Fremont had said the climate was wonderful and there were great opportunities for settlers. The leader of the party, generous old George Donner, was the first of a long line of retired farmers who wanted to go to California for the climate. Dozens of younger men, like James Reed, hoped to make their fortunes there. Virginia had plenty of friends to play with on the way — and no hostile Indians attacked the party.

THE DESERT RUN

After passing Bridger's Fort, Virginia began to feel very differently about her trip to California. The men

had endless trouble clearing a road so the heavy wagons could get over the mountains to the Great Salt Lake. Then there were two long waterless stretches of desert to cross before they reached the Sierra Nevada Mountains.

Many oxen died of thirst. Many wagons had to be left behind in the desolate, waterless waste. Virginia's parents lost almost everything they had started with. But worst of all, Virginia had to turn her back on Billy, her pony, who dropped in the hot sand from weariness, hunger and thirst.

The great mountains loomed ahead. People tried to hurry, because winter was coming, but worry and exhaustion made them quarrelsome. Then one day an awful thing happened.

Virginia's father saw a man beating a weary team of oxen, trying to make them pull harder than they could possibly pull.

"Stop that!" James Reed shouted in anger at the senseless cruelty.

"Shut up or I'll give you a taste of my whip!" the man threatened.

"Stop it, I say!"

Suddenly the man turned and began to use his whip on Reed. At that, Reed lost his temper completely and struck back — with a knife. When the fight ended, the ox driver was dead.

Virginia knew her father was a good man. He had never intended to kill the ox driver. She saw the three

great cuts that the whip had made in James Reed's head. She saw him throw his knife away in shame when he realized what he had done. But other members of the party were so desperate because of their great hardships on the desert crossing that they took out all their anger on James Reed. Furiously they drove him away from the wagon train. He'd have to go on to California by himself — if he could get there. And they sent him off without even letting him have a gun to shoot game he would need for food.

HELP FOR HER FATHER

Virginia watched her father ride off alone on Glaucus who was so thin now that he could scarcely carry his master.

"Something has to be done," Virginia told herself. "I can't let Father starve."

That night, when the people in camp were asleep, Virginia got up. She found a gun and ammunition, then slipped quietly away.

The barren country all around was good for one thing — Virginia could see the hoofprints that Glaucus had made. She followed her father's trail as fast as she could. If only Glaucus had been too tired to go far, things would be all right.

At last she found James Reed and gave him the gun.
Then she hurried back again to the wagon train before
she was missed. Virginia had saved the life of the stepfather whom she loved in spite of the terrible mistake he
had made.

WINTER COMES

The worst for Virginia and the other members of the
Donner party was yet to come. They reached the mountains too late. Snow covered the pass. The oxen and
horses could not pull any of the few wagons that were
left. The animals could not even plunge through the deep
snowdrifts with packs on their backs.

A small group of men went ahead for help. The rest of
the party had to stay in little log cabins that were hastily
built. Virginia, with her mother and sister and brothers,
waited day after day — week after week. What little food
they'd had disappeared. Soon many families had nothing
to eat but the skins of oxen or cows or horses. The Reed
children ate their dog.

People began to die of
starvation. Those who still
lived gave up hope that help
would ever reach them.
Many lost their minds.
Never, among all the pio-
neers, had men, women and
children suffered such hardships as those in the Donner
party.

WINTER RESCUE

James Reed found his way to California. So did a few others who left the Donner party and pushed ahead. At last rescuers floundered back over the mountains, bringing the little food they could carry on their backs.

Virginia and her five-year-old brother Johnny still had enough strength to travel. Helped by rescuers, they made their way through deep drifts and blizzards to the other side of the high mountains.

"Virginia!" The girl looked up and saw her beloved father on the trail. He had recovered from the cold and starvation of his trip into California. Now he was on his way back. As soon as he saw Virginia and Johnny were safe, James Reed left them. He had to help rescue her mother, her younger sister Patty and three-year-old Tommy.

No pioneer ever was more plucky than Virginia Reed, and no pioneer ever felt happier to reach the end of her journey. Somehow the whole Reed family managed to live through the dreadful winter and to reach the sunny Sacramento Valley.

The members of the Donner party happened to be from Illinois, and they had the same reasons for moving West that many people had. A few wanted to find a pleasant place in which to retire. Most of them were looking for a place where they might grow rich.

Other people in Illinois were forced to think of moving West. Their reasons were special. They were Mormons. They needed a place in which they could worship in a way they believed was right.

These Mormons had already made several moves in frontier country. Their church had started in western New York State, then moved to Ohio. People there had driven the Mormons out. The same thing happened again in Missouri.

After leaving Missouri, the Mormons settled in Illinois on the bank of the Mississippi River. There they worked hard and built up a prosperous community called Nauvoo. Then trouble once more surrounded the members of the Church of Jesus Christ of Latter-day Saints, which was the Mormons' official name for themselves.

Brigham Young

Brigham Young
and The Mormons

BRIGHAM YOUNG LOVED TO WALK about the town of Nauvoo, Illinois, with its comfortable houses of brick and stone and its huge Mormon church that people were building. He himself was a leader in the church, and he hoped that its members would be allowed to live here in their town undisturbed. But in the autumn of 1845 he grew sad, then angry at the terrible reports he heard. Groups of armed men kept attacking his friends who had built Nauvoo and made it into the biggest town west of Pittsburgh.

These lawless gangs disagreed with the Mormon religion, and they didn't believe in freedom of worship. But, more important than that, they wanted to drive the prosperous Mormons away so they could get their farms.

"My house and barn were burned today!" one man told Young.

"My cattle were killed!"

"My husband was shot!"

Brigham Young asked for protection from the officials of Illinois. No help came.

"We have to move away in order to save our lives," he said at last. "I have read Colonel Fremont's report of his

journey beyond the Rockies. Somewhere out there we will find the right place. We must settle where nobody else lives. We must find a new home where nobody will attack us."

By now winter had come and the Mississippi River was filled with ice. Young knew this was a bad time to lead twelve thousand people into the wilderness. Still, there was nothing else he could do. It would be a harder job than any pioneer had ever tried before. Where could all his people get food as they traveled? Where could thousands of horses and mules and oxen and milk cows find enough grass to eat?

"Somehow we will manage," he said grimly. "We have to, if we want to live."

THE MORMONS START THEIR TREK

Little ferryboats carried people, horses, cattle, wagons across the icy river. Bitter cold filled the tents that the Mormon people had to camp in, only seven miles from their warm homes. Many of them had no food at all for themselves or their animals. The armed mobs had destroyed their crops.

"We must share what we have," Young said.

They kept on sharing everything as the great wagon train started west in the spring. The prairie was so muddy, and the animals were so weak from hunger, that the caravan could travel only about two and a half miles a day. Brigham Young saw that he and his followers would die of starvation if they tried to push right on to the Rockies.

"There is only one thing to do," he announced. "We must stop and grow some food."

When they reached the Missouri River, the wagons stopped. People began to build log cabins and to plant crops. Here they would spend the winter, getting ready for the long trip across the plains.

Not everybody agreed with all of Brigham Young's decisions, but they had to admit he was a brave and sensible man. He had good ideas about little things as well as big ones, and that made him a remarkable leader indeed.

First of all, he kept every man, woman and child busy. Some of them made equipment and clothes for the journey that was still ahead of them. Others made milking stools and washboards and baskets that they could trade for food when they went past cabins along the way.

But it wasn't enough for twelve thousand people just to be busy. Brigham Young knew they had to be cheerful, too. Luckily, all the members of a brass band had joined the Mormon church, so Young arranged for band concerts at night. He organized dances and community sings. In spite of sickness and misery, the huge camp of log cabins and sod huts buzzed with activity. Everything went according to plans that Young worked out.

BRIGHAM YOUNG MEETS JIM BRIDGER

"Where are we going to settle?" the others kept asking Brigham Young.

Young wouldn't answer the question, but he did ask questions of his own when he pushed on with an advance party and began to meet Mountain Men.

"What about the country around the Salt Lake?" Young said to an old trapper who was called Peg Leg Smith.

"Nothing grows there, and there's no game," Peg Leg answered.

Still Young kept questioning.

"The Salt Lake country ain't fit to live in," Jim Bridger said.

Jim ought to know. He had discovered the Lake. Still, he was a trapper, not a farmer. He couldn't even understand why anyone would eat vegetables or bother with grain. Meat was the only decent food for a man. It was he who had bragged once that he hadn't tasted bread for seventeen years. And so, from his point of view, the Salt Lake region was no fit place to live.

"I'll give you a thousand dollars for the first bushel of wheat or the first ear of corn you grow there," he said to Brigham. Not that he would have touched wheat or corn if Young had brought any to him. It was just his way of saying the Mormons ought to find a better place to settle.

Young listened to these reports and instead of being dismayed he was delighted. But he was careful not to show it. For one thing he felt sure that Bridger and Peg Leg Smith didn't know what they were talking about. The soil was undoubtedly good for farming, because Fremont had said so. But, more important, it was good for the Mormons. Mountain Men warned everyone to stay away from the Salt Lake. This meant that if the Mormons settled there they would have the place to themselves. There would be no neighbors to bother them — which was exactly what the Mormons wanted most.

So Young turned his wagons into the rough trail that the Donner party had made just a short time before. Ahead of him lay the great unsettled land of Utah, which belonged to Mexico at that time. There the Mormons would make their new home.

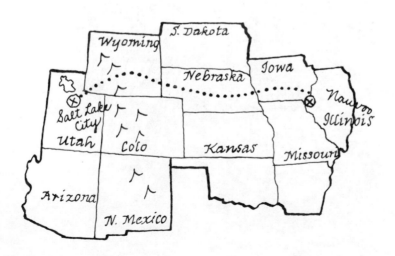

The Mormons were happy in Utah — except for one thing. They did not succeed in staying outside the United States.

The United States fought a war with Mexico and in 1848 won control of another huge section of the West. Utah was in that section. The place where the Mormons felt sure they would be safe from Americans who might bother them now belonged to the United States.

California also became part of the United States as a result of the Mexican War, and almost immediately something happened there which sent a new kind of pioneer hurrying toward the West.

Wagons Going West

"GOLD HAS BEEN DISCOVERED in California!"

This news spread in 1848 all over the eastern part of the United States with lightning speed. Thousands of men headed for the West Coast in covered wagons, on horseback, on foot. Some went in ships to Panama, then crossed overland through the jungle and took another ship up the coast.

A flood of people began pouring into the fabulous California country, which belonged to the United States now, instead of to Mexico. Because they went in 1849, the gold hunters came to be known as Forty-niners.

Many boys and girls crossed the Great Plains on the way to California in 1849 — and for years afterward. Some families made the trip alone or in little groups. But most people preferred to join one of the big wagon trains, with professional guides who knew how to deal with the problems they'd meet.

In the beginning, the Plains Indians were more surprised than alarmed by the white-topped prairie schooners. Then they began to realize what the endless stream of wagons meant. The pale-faced hordes were taking the Indians' hunting grounds. Already the buffalo, on which

the Plains Indians lived, were getting scarce. Tribe after
tribe fought bitterly to keep the white man off their lands.

Some people say it was Jim Bridger who first hit upon
the idea which turned out to be the wagon trains' best
method of defense against an Indian attack. Anyway,
most of the guides followed the plan. At night, or when
a battle threatened, drivers pulled their wagons up into a
great circle, with the front wheels cramped in toward the
center, so there was almost no space between one wagon
and the next. This made a kind of circular fort. Inside it
the cooking fires were built. Usually the horses and oxen
stayed in the circle for protection, too.

Now, if an Indian attack came, men could fire from
shelter. The bodies of the wagons absorbed arrows and
even bullets and saved many people's lives.

"THE ELEPHANT"

"Well, sir," said the guide to a couple of pioneer boys
one day, "here we are, with the Plains behind us. Are
you ready for The Elephant?"

"What!"

"You mean you don't know? Better find out," the
guide said with a grin.

"The Elephant," an oldtimer finally told the boys,
"why, that could be any number of things. When something's hard to do, we call it The Elephant."

This time, the guide meant the desert that had to be
crossed in Nevada, and it was no easier now than it had
been when the Donner party tackled it. So many wagons
were creaking toward California that they made an almost unbroken line. Prairie schooners from one party
were always getting mixed up with schooners from
another. Whole families, whose horses or mules had died,
often sat beside the trail, hoping that somebody would
give them a lift.

"Tonight we're going to chew The Elephant's ears," the guide told the two boys. "We'll have a little rest first."

Late that afternoon the boys filled the water barrels and the wagons started to roll. They were going to cross a strip of desert during the night, when it was cool. The boys watched the train go by for a while. One extra-large schooner had a privy built into it. Later they spied a man pulling a small handcart loaded with all his goods. Every time he passed a stalled wagon, he whinnied like a horse and asked how far it was to grass. Another man pushed a wheelbarrow and never spoke a word to anybody.

Just now The Elephant didn't seem too terrible. For a while the road had followed a river bank, and the boys had sneaked in a swim. They felt ready to walk all night with the men so the wagons would be as light as possible. By morning they were about as tired as human beings have ever been — but not too tired to see the body of a white man who had been scalped by Indians during the night. He had started a fight with the Indians, and they had left his body in plain view of the wagon trains as a warning that visitors in their land must behave themselves.

The night had been cold and the boys were glad when they stopped for breakfast. They helped chop up some abandoned wagons for fuel, and then had bacon and wheat cakes and coffee before they fell asleep.

At four o'clock in the afternoon the train started. By midnight the supply of water began to give out. Horses and mules were already frantic. Some of them stampeded when they heard the sound of splashing water as people poured drinks for themselves.

But the trip was not nearly over. It went on all night and the strain on the animals was terrible. Wagon wheels sank deep in the soft powdery stuff of the desert. Even at night the air was filled with choking dust. People tied handkerchiefs over their noses and mouths. But the animals had no such protection. By morning, when they reached solid ground that stretched ahead for a way, the entire train was ready for a long rest — but only a short pause for breath was possible. Half the desert lay ahead. If they wanted to get through alive they had to reach the Carson River that night.

"CALIFORNY, HERE WE COME"

The two boys staggered along beside the teams, wondering if they would ever make it. The legs and sides of the animals quivered with the endless strain of pulling. Their heads hung low — they were ready to lie down in the blazing heat and die.

Then, as people had almost given up hope, something like an electric shock went through the mules. Up came their heads. Their legs heaved with greater force against the yielding sand. They had smelled water. That could only mean that the Carson River was not far ahead. Soon team after panting team broke into a run as they gained solid ground on the edge of the desert.

At last they plunged crazily down a slope and into a great tangle of other wagons and teams that had charged into the water. People, too, ran for the river. In the muddy mess stirred up by hoofs and feet and wheels, they gulped water as fast as they could swallow. Some immediately grew very sick.

Hard as it was to control themselves, the boys did not drink at first. They walked upstream, where the water was clear, and lay down in it to cool off. When they were rested a little, they began to drink slowly and carefully.

At last they got up dripping and happy, with energy

enough for a great shout.

"We've chewed The Elephant's ears," they sang out. "Californy, here we come." They had proved they were men. They could take the worst the American continent had to offer. Now it didn't matter too much whether they got rich in the gold fields or not. That would depend on luck. Getting through the desert had depended solely on themselves. And they had done it.

William Downie

William Downie

WILLIAM DOWNIE WAS IN BOSTON when he heard the news of the rich gold discoveries in California. He decided to make the whole trip by sea. He was an experienced sailor, twenty-nine years old, and strong. He easily got a job on a vessel bound for San Francisco by way of Cape Horn.

Week after week the ship sailed south on a pleasant sea. Then for many days and nights, the ship fought terrible storms as she rounded the southern tip of South America. After that the weather grew pleasant again. Gentle winds filled the sails, and the ship moved steadily, but slowly, toward her goal.

There was nothing for William to do but work and wait and endure the months of boredom and the monotonous food — nothing but salt meat and hardtack. Sooner or later he would reach the goldfields. Meanwhile he was getting paid for going there.

Finally, one day in June the ship dropped anchor in San Francisco Bay.

One of the first things William saw was this sign hanging in front of a big tent: *Hotel — $16 per day*.

"No hotel for me!" William said.

William hunted for a place where he could throw down his blanket. He found it between two huge piles of cow hides that were waiting to be loaded on ships. "Hide Park," William called the spot. It was smelly, but it served as home for a few days while he looked for work. He needed more money than he had earned on the ship. Mining supplies were expensive. At last he found a job helping to load a ship that lay in the harbor.

WATERFRONT GANG

"Stay away from there!" some men yelled at William the next morning when he joined a group of sailors who were going to work on the same ship.

"Why should we stay away?" William asked.

The bullies laughed and showed their clenched fists.

"There's why!" they answered. Obviously they had been hired by some shipowner who wanted to keep cargo off anyone else's ship.

"Well, would you believe it!" William said, winking at his friends. "We've been hankering for a good living fight. Look out!"

The bullies gave one glance at the grinning sailors and disappeared among the shacks and tents on the waterfront.

This was William's first experience with frontier life. Soon he would see more of it when he bought his equipment and headed toward the diggings in the mountains.

SEARCH FOR GOLD

"Where's a good place to look for gold?" William asked every prospector he met.

No one would tell where he had found gold, although William could see that many men had it. They were using gold dust instead of money. Men in the raggedest clothes thought nothing of plunking down $12 worth of dust for a meal.

"Look here, young fellow," one prospector finally told William, "if there is one thing a miner don't care to talk about, it's where he's been. It's the same as a law here not to ask." Anyone who had discovered gold kept the location of his claim strictly to himself.

William gave up asking questions — but he didn't give up using his eyes and ears and wits. He wandered around in the mountains and managed to find a little of the precious metal. Then he had to quit mining and look for a doctor. He had injured a finger.

While he waited for the finger to heal, William set up a store in a tent. There he listened to the men who came in from the diggings.

One day two customers paid their bill with the biggest nuggets he had ever seen. Outside the tent the men had three mules, each with a very small pack. Why had such a small load been spread out on three mules, unless it was very heavy. The men pretended that their luck had been bad. They said they were going home in disgust — but William managed to get a pretty good idea of where they'd had all their "bad" luck.

That day he closed his store and started for this spot. On the way he tried to get men to go with him. But it was the wrong time of year. Most of the miners wanted to leave the mountains before winter set in.

Finally, William did locate some companions who needed work so much that they were willing to face the hardships of cold weather in the High Sierras. One was a boy, Mike Duvaney. One was a Moslem from sunny Egypt. The others were all Negroes, including a runaway slave, Albert Collis. Later a man called Hawaiian Jim, who had lived in California for a while, joined the party.

GOLD AT LAST

William led this group in the direction from which he was sure the giant nuggets had come. Ignoring all the advice he got along the way, he headed for the roughest country. There he found the canyon he was looking for.

Albert Collis kicked the gravel in the canyon bottom, and with his first kick a huge nugget appeared. Instantly the men attacked the gravel with any tools they could reach. Some even dug with butcher knives. They all found gold — lots of it. And they kept on finding it.

"I got sixteen ounces today," one man would report.

"I got twenty ounces," another said.

"Look at this — thirty ounces," came from a third.

Luck like this went on day after day. One morning the Egyptian went out to dig while the flapjacks were cooking. When he came in to breakfast he had forty ounces of gold.

"These diggings are played out," he complained. "I'm moving on." Anything could happen in this gold rush.

As gold piled up, food dwindled. The only man who knew the country was Hawaiian Jim, so he led several of the party back to the low country for supplies. Only Albert Collis, Charles Williams, Mike Duvaney and William Downie himself remained at the diggings.

STARVING RICH MEN

Day after day in freezing weather they panned more gold and waited for food. The little bit of flour left in the sack was now more precious than all their gold. But with nothing else to do while they waited, the three men and one boy kept on piling up gold even though they were growing weaker and weaker from hunger. Finally Albert Collis became so weak he couldn't walk.

"Hawaiian Jim must have lost his way," William told the others. "I'll go down to find him and bring back food."

At the first mining camp he reached, William found

men who were as hungry as he and his companions. The whole camp was living on soup made from the bones of a cow they had found dead — and those bones had been boiled over and over for days.

William had enough gold with him to buy a whole grocery store, but he couldn't find even a bite of food at any price. Then he had a stroke of luck. He met a train of heavily-laden horses struggling through wet snow. Many of the packs on these horses contained food. William bought all he could, even though the food was soaking wet. Then he began the return journey.

All along the way he had kept asking about Hawaiian Jim. No one had seen or heard of the fellow.

William needed help with the horses he had bought. The only man he could hire was about the meanest looking customer on seven continents. But William had no choice. The big job now was to keep this helper from stealing the horses and food. Somehow William managed this, and he got back to camp in time to save the lives of his companions.

It was bitter hard work panning gold that winter. The water often turned to ice in the pan before the gravel had been washed away from the gold. But William and his three companions kept working.

LOW-DOWN MISSOURIANS

Then spring came, and with it came other miners. One day William heard one of the newcomers talking to himself.

"Those dirty, low-down Missourians," the man kept saying over and over as he dug in the gravel on his claim.

"What's wrong with people from Missouri?" William wanted to know.

"They're no good — bring bad luck," the miner grumbled.

"What in the world did Missourians do to you that makes you so sore at them?" William asked.

"I just tried to sell this claim to some of them," the angry miner explained. "To make it look worth buying, I buried three ounces of gold in the sand. Then I showed these good-for-nothing Missourians where to dig. Know what they did? They dug somewhere else — and covered up my gold so I can't even find it myself. A Missourian is the poorest excuse for a human being of any critter in God's whole green world."

Downie laughed and moved on. A few days later the Missouri-hating miner struck it rich on the very claim where he had buried his three ounces of gold. Things like that kept happening in the diggings.

A GOOD TURN

As good weather came, William's companions began to get restless. Like all gold-seekers they weren't satisfied with what they had. They wanted to look for even richer gravel.

William couldn't leave because he was nursing a sick prospector who had come to stay in his cabin. William even slept on the floor so the man could have his bed.

When the invalid recovered and was able to travel, William had an idea.

"Will you do a favor for me?" he asked.

"Do anything in the world for you, the way you've treated me," the man replied.

"Will you take my gold down to Sacramento and sell it and put the money in the bank?" William asked. "Since you're going anyway, it would be a real help."

"Sure thing," the man said, and soon he was on the trail with $20,000 worth of nuggets.

That was the last William heard of the sick prospector — or the gold — until one day much later when a message came from Panama. The man who had gone off with William's $20,000 sent his kindest regards.

All the work of a long terrible winter had gone for nothing, but William was determined to try again. While

he was buying supplies he ran into Hawaiian Jim, the fellow who had gone for food at the beginning of winter and never returned.

"Where have you been and why didn't you bring back food?" William demanded.

Hawaiian Jim looked thoroughly surprised and frightened.

"I thought you were dead," he managed to say.

"You mean you left us to starve to death," William replied. "You were planning to go back to our camp and pick up our gold!"

Hawaiian Jim didn't deny the accusation. He just suddenly disappeared among the jungle of tents in the mining camp. William Downie didn't waste time trying to find him. Instead he shrugged, packed his supplies and headed for new diggings.

Gold made criminals of some men, but it had a different effect on others. It helped them to have interesting ideas. For example, it made young Edward Beale think he would like to bring some camels to America!

Beale had charge of the first packtrain that took gold from California to the East. As he drove thirsty, weary horses and mules through the desert, he kept saying to himself, "There ought to be an easier way of doing this."

But how could he make the job easier?

Beale didn't know at first. The idea didn't come until a little later when he was in desert country again. This time he was with Kit Carson exploring Death Valley in California. Death Valley had earned its name. Many men and a great many horses and mules and oxen died trying to cross it. The heat was terrible. There was no grass for the animals, and worst of all there was no water for either man or beast.

As Beale and Carson explored Death Valley, they carried with them both water and food for the animals. This was a great nuisance, because it meant taking care of many extra mules.

The bare, dry country made Beale think of a book he had read about travelers in Asia who crossed a desert but did not have any of the trouble he was having. The reason was obvious. They rode camels instead of horses and they carried their baggage on camels. These beasts were very strong. They could eat desert plants that a mule or horse wouldn't touch, and they could go great distances without water.

Why not bring camels into the West?

Beale went back East to Washington, and there he told his idea to the Secretary of War. This gentleman, it turned out, had already thought of the same thing. The Secretary was Jefferson Davis, and he had special reasons for wanting good transportation in the West.

Jefferson Davis had big ambitions for the part of the United States that he came from, the South. He liked the southern system of growing cotton on big plantations, where there were many slaves to do the work. He hoped this system would spread westward. The climate in the Southwest was right for cotton-growing. Only one thing was lacking. There was no good way to get the cotton to a seaport on the nearest coast, which was in California.

Jefferson Davis thought camels might be able to do this job. He decided to find out how camels would get along in the Southwest.

Men went to distant lands to buy camels and hire drivers who knew how to handle them. Edward Beale was going to be in charge of the first American camel expedition. While he waited for the animals to arrive, he took a vacation in the small town of Chester, Pennsylvania.

Edward Beale

Camels Go West

THREE BOYS WHO LIVED IN CHESTER pestered their parents a good deal during the winter of 1856-57. They wanted to travel through the Indian country of the Southwest with Edward Beale's camel expedition.

The boys were Hampden Porter (Ham for short), Joseph Bell (Joe, of course), and a member of the Stacey family whose first name was unusual for a boy. It was May.

Ham, Joe and May all knew and admired Edward Beale. He had been a Lieutenant in the Navy, then an explorer, then Superintendent of Indian Affairs in far-off Nevada and California. Naturally, while Beale visited in Chester he talked about his plan to cross the desert with camels. Naturally, the boys wanted to go with him. In the end their parents agreed, and the boys started for Texas where the camels were to land.

Traveling first by railroad, they went to Pittsburgh. Then they took a steamboat down the Ohio and Mississippi rivers and on to the coast of Texas. Then they rode inland on horses. Finally they reached their destination, a ranch outside the town of San Antonio. The boys all knew that was where Davy Crockett had died fighting at the Alamo.

By now the camels had also arrived in Texas. The big awkward-looking animals had come by ship all the way from Turkey. On the ship they had caused no trouble, except that one of them was so big that sailors had to cut a hole in the deck above where he stood. They had to make room for his hump!

The camels were not actually at the ranch when Ham, Joe and May arrived. They were away getting a load of supplies, but in the early evening the boys heard a strange jingle of bells. In the twilight they saw twenty-five camels, each one with a string of bells looped around its curved neck. Along with the jingling came other strange sounds. These were the orders that the Turkish, Greek and Armenian camel drivers gave in some foreign tongue.

The three boys were excited. An uproar in the nearby corrals showed that the mules and horses were even more excited. They reared and snorted and dashed from one side to another as if their very lives were threatened.

The dignified camels paid no attention to the unimportant little mules and horses. They just quietly doubled their long legs under them and settled down on the ground so that the drivers could take the tremendous loads off their backs.

In the morning the boys examined the camels more closely. Compared with horses and mules these beasts had enormous feet, and their backs were different, too. One was a dromedary. He had a single big hump on his back. The others all had double humps.

The boys tried sitting in a queer saddle that fitted on the dromedary's back. Then they took turns riding. The motion the animal made was very different from the familiar, easy gait of horses, and the rough, unpleasant gait of mules. The way the camels carried loads was surprising too. The biggest camel could rise from his knees with more than half a ton on his back. Since the boys were going to have to help tie packs on the camels, they spent as much time as they could learning how to do this.

There wasn't much time, though, to learn anything. The expedition got started very soon. First in the line of march were covered wagons, each pulled by a team of six mules. Next came extra mules and extra horses, driven along by men who rode horses. After these came the biggest of the camels. His name was Mahomet and he was the natural leader of the others. They strung out behind him — sometimes far behind. The whole procession made a beautiful sight as it stretched out over the prairie.

At first the boys feared that the camels could never make the journey. They lagged far behind. They seemed exhausted after each day's trip. But the beasts were merely out of condition. They had done no work on their long sea voyage. Soon they were keeping up easily with the mules and horses. In the very dry plains of western Texas the camels even helped the horses and mules. They did this by carrying kegs of water for them to drink.

Along the way were signs that white men and Indians

had fought here just a year or two before. Sometimes the boys thought they saw Indians, although Edward Beale was sure there were none around. Still Beale took no chances. He had men stand guard every night.

Ham, Joe and May were delighted when they reached a village where Mexicans lived. The people seemed to think a circus had come to town. Children asked if there were any trained dogs. The boys didn't want to disappoint them. They kept straight faces while one of them said, "No, we have no trained dogs. But some of our horses can drink out of bottles while they are standing on their heads."

One old Mexican was very eager to have the camels camp beside his own village farther along. He offered to give the party all the eggs and onions they could eat if they would stay there over night.

Occasionally, one or another of the boys got a chance to ride Seid, the dromedary. He could travel long distances faster than any horse. The boys wished there were more dromedaries. They were tired of riding cranky mules. More than once the ornery critters had bucked them off and run away. The dromedary never bucked. In fact, none of the camels ever caused trouble. Patiently, quietly, they did any work they were ordered to do. Sometimes when a mule team got stuck on a steep hill,

the powerful camels would pull a wagon right to the top.
Sometimes the mules would have trouble when they came
to sand. Their small hooves sank right down into it. The
camels, with their big feet, could walk on top of the sand.
So the drivers would hitch them up and let them pull the
wagons until they reached solid ground. Also, wherever
they were, the camels seemed to find food for themselves.
Anything seemed to agree with them, and they could go
for days without water.

At one Indian village Beale bought a hundred sheep.
Now the caravan made a greater spectacle than ever.
Although the boys had to work hard taking care of the
sheep they were glad to have them along. Each night a
sheep was butchered and roasted. This way they had
fresh meat. Mutton was a welcome change from salt
bacon which was the only meat the expedition had
started out with.

The timid sheep brought excitement, too. Panthers
sometimes tried to sneak into camp to get a little meat
for themselves. The guards now had to watch out for
these big cats as well as for hostile Indians.

No matter what kind of land they crossed, or how hard
the traveling, the camels seemed to like it. They grew
stronger as the horses and mules grew weaker.

By now the boys were very proud of the big, amiable
beasts. Ham, Joe and May cheered for the camels against
the horses and mules. When the expedition came to the
Colorado River, between Arizona and California, the
camels proved they were champions.

No one knew whether or not the camels could swim.
The river was wide and swift. Ten horses and mules
drowned, trying to cross. Then old Mahomet led the
other camels into the muddy, rough water, and they all
acted as if they were on a holiday spree. Some of them

swam upstream against the powerful current just for the fun of it. And they all got across without the slightest trouble.

The camels had passed the final test. Surely, Edward Beale thought, these wonderful animals would take the place of horses and mules in many parts of the West. Ham and Joe and May all agreed enthusiastically.

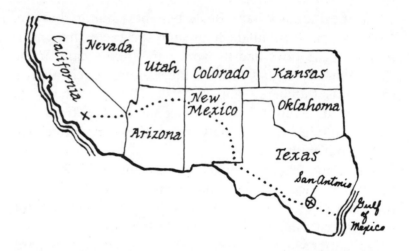

Other people thought so too. Camels came from China to carry ore out of the mines in the Nevada desert. Some camels made another journey across Arizona, from west to east. Others were used on various jobs in California. But they never did become the great load-carriers in the West.

This wasn't the camels' fault. The Civil War interrupted all experiments with them. Then after the Civil War, railroads spread very quickly, and even the most enthusiastic camel fans had to admit that railroads were better at carrying loads.

Soon, almost the only camels left in America were a few solemn beasts that appeared in circuses. But every once in a while a prospector moving through the California desert would rub his eyes and decide the heat had got him. He couldn't believe what he saw—but he should have.

For many years there actually were a few bands of runaway camels in the desert. Whenever Ham and Joe and May heard reports about them they recalled the wonderful journey they had taken, perhaps with these very camels. They, and Edward Beale, were sad when they heard that bullets and bows and arrows had killed the last of the wild camels in America.

Edward Beale's expedition started in Texas. If rail-roads hadn't been built, camels might have become as much a part of the scenery of that state as horses and long-horned cattle. But after the Civil War, broncs and beef critters had Texas all to themselves — except, of course, for cowboys.

Charlie Siringo

Charlie Siringo

LITTLE CHARLIE SIRINGO, WHO HAD NO CLOTHES to his name except a shirt made out of a flour sack, watched every move of the strange men called cowboys. He saw how they chased the quick longhorn cattle along the Texas coast where he lived. He studied the way they roped the beasts, tied them, and put a brand on them with a hot iron.

"I'm going to be a cowboy!" Charlie decided. And, as soon as he was big enough, he got a job with an outfit near the coast. Longhorns were everywhere, running wild. During the Civil War ranchers and cowboys had gone off to fight, so the animals had run loose and multiplied. Anybody could have them now — if he could catch them. Ships waited in the harbors to carry either the animals or their hides to market in Boston or New York.

"Chuck!" the cook bellowed every morning about two hours before sunrise in the cow camp where Charlie Siringo first worked.

"Breakfast!" the boss yelled right after him. "Get up, you lazy good-for-nothings!"

After steaming hot coffee, meat and biscuits, Charlie saddled his pony. By the time it was light enough to see,

he had ridden out on the prairie where cattle were graz-
ing peacefully. He had to round them up fast, because
at sunrise they were sure to disappear into the thick,
shady brush.

All day, Charlie rode back and forth, keeping the critters herded together out in the open. Sometimes he had
trouble with one of the big old steers, which were called
mossyhorns because moss actually grew on their horns.
These old fellows were the natural leaders in a herd.
They often tried to start a stampede back into the brush.

Gradually the cowboys in his outfit rounded up a big
herd that they could drive toward the waiting ships. Day
after day Charlie followed this routine until he became
as expert as any old hand. Now he could get a job anywhere in the West.

UP THE CHISHOLM TRAIL

Before long cowboys stopped driving the herds to the
Texas coast. Railroads were built to Kansas. Now trains
could carry live animals to market faster than ships
could. So the cowpokes began driving huge herds of long-

horns for a thousand or fifteen hundred miles to the railroad. Eighteen-year-old Charlie Siringo found that this
was a man-sized job.

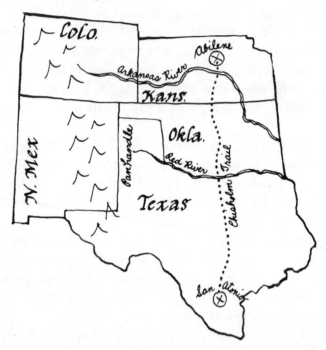

For a month he rode all day every day, helping to
round up the critters. Half of every night he spent riding
in a circle around the herd to keep it from scattering or
running away. As he circled slowly he used a cowboy
trick to soothe the nervous cattle. He sang them songs.

Charlie was dog-tired when it came time to drive a
thousand steers to Kansas along the Chisholm Trail. This
really wasn't a narrow trail at all. It was a route, sometimes half a mile or even a mile wide, along which the
slow-moving riders drove the longhorns. It had to be
wide, for cattle traveled over it by the millions, and they
needed grass to eat along the way.

The first night out on the trail, the critters were rest-less. They began to drift — or "slide"— away from camp. Charlie was singing away to quiet them when all at once an inexperienced cowboy galloped up.

"Let 'em slide! We'll stay with 'em!" he shouted boast-fully, and galloped straight into the herd. The frightened animals scattered in wild stampede. Charlie followed one bunch and finally got it stopped. Again he sang what he called "melodious" songs until the beasts all lay down to sleep.

By now Charlie was about worn out. He hooked his right leg over the saddle horn, held the reins in his right hand, and lay back with his left elbow on the horse's rump and his head in his left hand. Resting like that, he proceeded to take a nap.

Suddenly the nervous longhorns stampeded again. Be-fore Charlie could straighten up, his frightened horse took off and ran away. Still lying stretched out with his leg around the saddlehorn, he managed to stay aboard till he got the horse stopped.

It took the rest of the night and all the next day to round up the scattered critters. Then came a storm with thunder and lightning. That night, too, the cowboys sat up with the steers to keep them from stampeding. Next morning, with no sleep at all for two days, Charlie just mounted a fresh horse, and the trail drive went on.

ROPING A BUFFALO

"Charlie, ride out and turn the critters back," the trail boss said one evening when he saw some longhorns stray-ing from the herd.

Charlie saddled up quickly and went off, leaving his gun and pistol in camp. Just as he got the cattle rounded up, a big herd of buffalo stampeded by.

"Buffalo hump ribs would be a mighty good change

from beef," Charlie said to himself, and he galloped off after them. It was a long chase. But finally the buffalo stopped from exhaustion and stood panting with their big tongues hanging out.

"Easy enough to get one now," Charlie thought. He reached for his gun. Only then did he realize that he'd come off without it. Without his pistol, too. Even his bowie knife was missing. It hung from the belt that held the pistol.

"I'll rope one," he decided and lost no time opening a good loop in his lariat. A minute later he had a husky calf tugging at the end of the rope.

"Now how am I going to kill the critter?" Charlie asked himself. The only weapon he had was a rusty old pocketknife he'd found somewhere. First he tried to break the calf's neck by running his horse, then stopping short with a jerk on the rope. But the calf was too tough. He tried throwing it, the way he would a steer. The nimble creature was on its feet each time before he could tie its legs. But at last he got it down and lashed its feet together with a silk scarf he used for a belt on his pants.

It was a tough job to slaughter the calf with the small blade of the pocketknife (the big blade was broken). It was even tougher to skin it. Charlie wanted that skin to show the boys in camp. It would be quite a feather in his cap to bring back a skin when everybody knew he had no weapons on him.

With a choice hunk of meat wrapped up in the skin and tied behind the saddle, Charlie started back. All of a sudden he realized how far he had come. He'd have to spend the night on the prairie. Now he was glad he had the skin. It would do for a blanket.

Spreading it on the ground, flesh side down, Charlie went to sleep. But not for long. In no time at all thousands of ants, attracted to the fresh skin, were crawling all over him. Charlie got up and away from there in a hurry, and when he lay down again he left the skin on his saddle.

The cowboys had something to talk about next night when Charlie caught up with them twenty miles farther along the trail.

BILLY THE KID

Later, when Charlie had more experience, he got a job on the LX Ranch in the flat western part of Texas that is called the Panhandle.

"Charlie," the boss said to him one day, "You take some men and go over into New Mexico. I want you to get back the critters that Billy the Kid's been rustling off me."

"It might take all winter," Charlie said.

"I don't care if it does. Stay till you get these critters or bust."

So Charlie set out with men from the LX and from other ranches, too. They hadn't been in New Mexico long before they found the LX brand on some hides in a slaughterhouse. Asking cautious questions, Charlie traced the hides to a wealthy rancher who was buying cattle that Billy the Kid stole in Texas.

In time Charlie collected enough evidence to put that big rancher out of the cattle-rustling business. This was exciting work, so Charlie changed from rounding up cattle to rounding up men who stole cattle. He became a pioneer law man.

Men who enforced the law came along behind other kinds of pioneers. In one way they marked the end of the frontier, but pioneering didn't stop just because law and order arrived. The spirit of adventure and discovery in men is too strong to let that happen.

The more men learned about the West, the more they wanted to know. The pioneer spirit stayed very much alive. The story of John Wesley Powell shows what happened.

John Wesley Powell

John Wesley Powell

WHEN JOHN WESLEY POWELL WAS NINE YEARS OLD, his mother decided it wasn't safe for him to go to the log-cabin school near their home in southern Ohio. Every day some of the other boys threw stones at Wes, and Mrs. Powell was afraid that they would cripple or kill him.

Wes knew very well why the boys were after him. They believed in slavery. Wes's father was a minister who preached against slavery. He was an Abolitionist.

To make matters worse, Reverend Powell was away from home preaching in distant towns when the stone-throwing got particularly dangerous. So Mrs. Powell went to a neighbor, Big George Crookham, to get his advice. Big George was just as much an Abolitionist as Reverend Powell, and he wanted to help. Luckily, he could give the best kind of help at that moment. He ran a school in a log cabin on his farm. It was a free school for grown men who had never had a chance to get much education. Big George said he would be very glad to have Wes come there for lessons, too.

So it happened that Wes was the only boy in a school for grownups. He liked it. Most of all he liked a log-cabin

museum that stood next to the class-
room. In it were specimens of all the
plants and rocks in the neighborhood. Also, there were arrowheads,
tools, and decorations made by ancient Indians who had built mysterious mounds along the Ohio
River.

Wes spent long happy days learn-
ing all he could from these collections. Then suddenly
his regular classes ended. Pro-slavery bullies burned down
the museum and schoolroom.

But Big George went right on teaching Wes. They took
long walks together in the woods and ravines nearby.
Sometimes another teacher went along — a man who was
the state geologist of Ohio. From these two men who
loved science, Wes learned more about nature than he
could have learned in any school in the United States.
Few colleges even taught science in 1843, the year when
Wes was also learning that all men should be free, with
equal chances in the world.

"Have you ever seen a railroad?" Big George asked
on one of their walks far from home.

"Yes," Wes answered.

"All right, but now I'll show you a kind of railroad
you *haven't* seen," Big George said, and he pointed to
some caves in a rock ledge along the side of a ravine.

Wes looked with wonder at three men who crawled
out of one of the caves. They were unlike any he had
ever seen before. They were black. Wes had heard a
great deal about slavery, but he had never before seen a
Negro.

The men greeted Big George and talked with him in

soft, excited voices. On the way home, Big George explained that they were escaped slaves. The cave was their hiding place — a station on the secret road to freedom known as the Underground Railroad.

BATTLES AND FOSSILS

Before long the Powell family moved away from southern Ohio and on farther to the west. Wes managed to get a few more years of schooling, but it was never as exciting as what he learned from Big George about science — and about democracy. When the Civil War broke out, he enlisted in the Union Army. He worked hard and soon became an officer. For a while he commanded a company of former slaves who wanted to fight for an end to all slavery.

One day when he was commanding other troops, he went into battle at a place in Tennessee called Shiloh. He put up his right hand in a signal for his men to charge. At that instant a bullet shattered his upraised arm. The wound was so bad that the arm had to be cut off above the elbow. But Wes Powell refused to leave the army. He went on soldiering, and he found time for science, too.

Once he spied some fossils in a trench his men were digging, directly under the Confederate guns during the great battle at Vicksburg, Mississippi. Wes picked up a whole collection of the fossils and shipped them home to study after the war was over.

Wes was a good soldier. He had enlisted as a private and he ended up a major. He did important work in the army, so he met important generals. One of them was Ulysses S. Grant, who later became President. Another was John C. Fremont, the famous explorer who told him there were great areas of the West that were still unknown.

After the war ended, Powell decided to take a look at the West. First he followed the known trails. In 1867, he climbed Pike's Peak, just as Edwin James had done forty-seven years before. Wes had a wife now. Emma was her name, and she climbed Pike's Peak with him. Emma Powell was the first woman who got to the top, and she made the whole climb wearing a long skirt and three long petticoats!

Next year Wes Powell led the first party that ever climbed Long's Peak in Colorado. The other men were all glad they had two hands as they inched along knife-ledge ridges and clung to the face of great sloping rocks. Somehow Wes managed to do everything with only one hand.

The melting snow on Long's Peak interested Powell. It ran off in little streams that met in a bigger stream and rushed away down the great mountain. On the western side of the mountain Powell knew that he was looking at one of the sources of the Colorado River. The pure clear water from Long's Peak — and a thousand other peaks — ended far away in the Gulf of Mexico, brown and thick with mud.

By now several explorers had crossed the Colorado River at different places. Escalante had crossed it twice — once near its upper end and once hundreds of miles farther south where it flowed at the bottom of a huge canyon. Other men had looked down at it from the tops of canyon walls at other places. The river, like a giant buzz saw, had cut its way deep into rock for a long way, but no one knew exactly where it ran through an area five hundred miles long and two hundred miles wide. On maps this whole region was marked "unknown." The Colorado River might twist and turn and flow for a thousand miles to cover a distance that was only half that long, as the crow flies.

The more he thought about the Colorado the more curious Wes grew. Where did it go? Through what kind of country did it run? What could be learned by studying the layers of rock in the canyon walls that other explorers said were a mile deep in places? Could men travel down the Colorado? No one could answer even this very simple question about the river, and the more Powell explored around its headwaters, the more he felt he could never be satisfied until he found out.

GETTING READY

Powell prepared carefully for an expedition down the river. The journey he planned would have to be slow, because he wanted to stop and study the country all along the way. Ten months seemed about the right time to allow. This meant that the explorers had to carry with them enough food, clothing and other equipment for ten months. And they had to take it all in boats on a river that would probably be very rough and dangerous.

Powell designed four special boats for the journey. Three of them were very strong. They could carry heavy loads, and they had airtight compartments that would keep them from sinking if they should fill up with water. The fourth boat was small and light. It would carry Powell and two oarsmen downstream ahead of the others to see if the heavy boats could follow safely.

The boats had to be made in far-off Chicago. Then they came west on flat cars on the transcontinental railroad that was just being completed. As a matter of fact, the boats reached the Green River in Wyoming on May 12, 1869, just one day after the final rail was laid in the road that ran all the way from the Atlantic to the Pacific coast.

The Green River flowed into the Colorado, so Powell started his expedition under the railroad bridge that crossed it. At his camp under the bridge, Powell collected a crew of nine men besides himself. One member was his brother Walter who had also been an officer in the Union Army. Five were experienced Mountain Men. One of them, the cook, was called Billy Rhodes when Powell first met him. Later on, Billy confessed that his real name was William Rhodes Hawkins, but he liked to forget the Hawkins part, because he was wanted by the law back in Missouri.

A man named Adams wanted to join the party. Everybody, including Wes Powell, tried to discourage him, but he couldn't take a hint. He hung around, putting on airs and acting as if he was the real boss of the expedition. According to Billy Hawkins, it was he — Billy — who had the brilliant idea that finally got rid of Adams.

One night the members of the party sat around while two pots simmered on the campfire in the center of the circle. In one pot was coffee and in the other, some laundry.

A Mountain Man filled his cup with coffee and took a sip.

"This tastes mighty queer," he grumbled.

Billy Hawkins, who was cook, went to the fire to investigate. He peered into the pots, then poked his hunting knife into one of them and lifted out a dirty sock. From where Adams sat, it looked as if the sock came from the coffeepot. His interest in the expedition ended then and there.

A few days after the first transcontinental train crossed the bridge overhead, a small crowd of people came to watch the beginning of the first expedition down the Colorado River. Powell led the way in the small boat which he called the "Emma" after his wife. No one knew what kind of trouble he might find. There might be great waterfalls. Rumors told of giant whirlpools or "sucks," where boats would be pulled down, never to come up again.

DOWN THE COLORADO

Sometimes the boats barely moved along, because the stream was very sluggish. This meant long days of hard, monotonous rowing. Other times the boats raced as fast as a railroad train — and in water that dashed between canyon walls, roaring with a sound very much like that of a train. Now the men had to pull hard on the oars and steer with big sweeps to keep the boats from smashing into rocks and then turning over in the churning water.

It was May 30 when the boats entered a spectacular canyon that Powell called Flaming Gorge because of the

brilliant color of the cliff walls. Writing with the left hand he had learned to use for everything, he put this down in his diary: "Old mountaineers tell us the river here cannot be run."

The boats did make the run. Then they came to a violent rapids. An old Indian had told Powell about an attempt to go down this stretch of river in a bullboat, which the Indians called a "water-pony."

"The water go hoo-woogh, hoo-woogh," the old Indian said. "Water pony buck. Water catch 'em. No see Indian any more."

The white explorers managed to pass this spot. But a few days later some of the men did get bucked into the water. Their boat, called the "No-Name," was smashed to pieces, and one-third of the supplies for the ten-month ⁀ disappeared in the muddy river.

⁀ ⁀ngs in the other boats got wet and spoiled. When ⁀ Billy Hawkins called out "Plunder, plunder, ⁀ ⁀t it," there was less and less food to come

⁀men could catch fish. Once in a while ⁀n sheep on the canyon wall. But ⁀men grew very thin and very

Time and again the boats had to be unloaded and carried empty along the shore past waterfalls. Other times the men walked along the shore and let the boats float down, tied to long ropes. Once the current was so powerful it pulled a boat away from them and the rope burned their hands as it slipped through. The men had a long walk along the rocky shore before they found the boat stuck on a sand bar.

Powell could not help with the work that took t[...] hands, but there was plenty of climbing for him to d[...] he explored the canyon walls. Once he and another [...] ber of the expedition decided to find out how far [...] from the canyon bottom to the rim. The other m[...]

George Bradley, and the important thing to remember about him is the way he was dressed. He wore buckskin leggins over long underwear.

Now here is the story, almost as Powell wrote it down that night in his diary:

"We climbed six or eight hundred feet, then we were met by a sheer precipice. Looking about, we found a place where it seemed possible to climb. I went ahead. Bradley followed. We proceeded until we were nearly to the summit. Here by making a spring, I gained a foothold in a little crevice, and grasped an angle of the rock overhead. I found I could get up no farther, and could not step back, for I did not dare to let go my hand, and could not reach a foothold below without doing so.

"I called to Bradley for help. He found a way by which he could get to the top of the rock over my head, but he could not reach down to me. He looked around for a stick or a limb of a tree, but he could not find one."

All this time Powell had been standing on his toes, and his legs began to tremble with the strain.

"I knew if I lost my hold I should fall to the bottom. . . ."

At this instant Bradley had an idea. He took off his buckskin leggins and then his drawers, which were longer and stronger than the leggins. He swung the drawers down over the cliff. Powell hugged close to the rock, let go with his hand, seized the dangling legs, and held on while Bradley pulled him to the top.

Powell was saved from death — and by a suit of long underwear — but this is what he wrote next in his diary: "Then we walked out on a jutting rock and made the necessary observations for determining its altitude above camp."

Powell was like that. He refused to let dangers and difficulties stand in his way.

The last part of his exploration had to be done faster than he wanted, because food had run out, but Powell finished the job anyway. However, three of his men got so hungry and so frightened by the river that they quit the expedition a few days before the end of the journey. They climbed up the canyon wall. On top they met Indians and had some misunderstanding with them. Nobody ever found out exactly what happened, except that the three white men were killed.

MORE PIONEERING

A single trip down the Colorado didn't satisfy Powell. There was still a tremendous amount to learn. For nine years he continued to explore the area or to direct the explorations of others. Then he went on to different things that were of great importance to his fellow Americans.

Powell became a pioneer in getting the government to support the work of scientists. He had made his first great river voyage without any government help, except for free food that came from the Army. It seemed to him that scientists ought to have more than that. So he went to Washington and talked to congressmen. He argued. He made speeches. He persuaded, and at last he won. The government set up special scientific agencies. One of these was the Bureau of Reclamation, which was supposed to save water and land in the dry West.

Powell was made head of the United States Geological Survey, another government agency. The Survey mapped the country and studied its rocks for any signs of minerals that might be useful.

In addition to all this, Powell persuaded men in Washington to support a new science — the science of the study of man. He established the Bureau of American Ethnology with government aid, and he headed it for many years. People in this Bureau were particularly interested in Indians, as Powell himself had been from the day when he first saw the arrowheads and tools in Big George Crookham's log-cabin museum. When Powell met Ute Indians in the West, he learned their language. Later, while his teams of surveyors studied the canyon of the Colorado, Powell often went off to study the Utes or the Paiutes or the Hopis. He became an authority on their stories and legends, and on the folklore and languages of Indians in general.

The ever-pioneering John Wesley Powell was a leader of men on the frontier of science. He never finished college, but he lived to be president of the American Association for the Advancement of Science.

Conclusion

The frontiersmen were out in front. Pioneering meant being first. Pioneers were the ones who began. They started things. So, any story of pioneers is a story of beginnings, and beginnings go on and on. Men are always making discoveries and learning to live in new ways.

Pioneering has never stopped since the day when Daniel Boone rode a horse along the Warriors Path into Kentucky. The modern pilot who first crossed the West in a jet plane was very much a pioneer too. And men are still pioneering. They do this in many different ways in many different parts of the world. They cross Antarctica just as Lewis and Clark once crossed America. They go down to deep ocean bottoms as Edwin James once climbed to the top of Pike's Peak. They orbit the earth in capsules and look out with wonder on space, as Jim Bridger once sat in a bullboat on the Bear River just to see where it went.

The pioneer spirit of the Old West lives on in the world today. Pioneers now, as in the past, live exciting lives on the edge of the future.

Index

247

920
Fo

Copy 1

AUTHOR

Folsom, Franklin

TITLE

Famous Pioneers

DATE LOANED	BORROWER'S NAME	DATE RETURNED
1-24-69	Cindy moore	
	Lee Levine	1-29-69
	Mari Haugh	
	Kenneth	

920
Fo

Copy 1

Folsom, Franklin

Famous Pioneers